Conquer And Control Your Money

Secrets That Will Change Your Life

Alan Fensin

Published by Burlington Books Div.
Burlington National Inc.
Box 841, Mandeville, LA 70470
United States of America
http://www.conquerandcontrol.com

The information in this book comes from highly regarded sources. Although reasonable efforts were made to publish reliable information, the author and the publisher assume no responsibility for the material or any consequences of its use.

Copyright © 2014 by Alan Fensin.
All rights reserved.
No part of this book shall be reproduced, stored in a retrieval system or transmitted by any means, electronic, mechanical, photocopying, recording or otherwise, without first obtaining written permission from the publisher.

Library of Congress Control Number: 2014915696

ISBN 978-1-57706-670-5
Printed in the United States of America.

WHAT PEOPLE ARE SAYING ABOUT CONQUER AND CONTROL

This accessible and well-developed book brings your subconscious mind out of the shadows to help you solve money problems. —John Toomey

Conquer and Control isn't some feel-good, just be positive stuff. It is a logical and practical formula that you can apply to the money problems you want to get rid of. —Joseph Keene

A pioneering and invaluable work about how to change bad habits. —Chester Imperato

This book offers indispensable practical methods to change some really bad money problems. —Bill Malone

The *Conquer and Control* strategies are much more powerful than just using will power. Properly executed, the *Conquer and Control* principles will drastically improve your life. —Allen Brusiewski

If you want to improve your money consciousness, this book is invaluable. Get it and use it! —Jim Locke

Buy this book. You won't be disappointed - it will change your life. —Robert LaPierre

Fensin boils down years of money research to give us proven methods to change our destructive habits. —Bob Porter

This book takes us on a tour of our subconscious mind and shows us how to exert conscious control to change it and stop our bad money habits. —Bert Phillips

Lots of books tell you what you should do, but this book shows you how to do it. —Raymond Cuomo

This is a fascinating look into the workings of the subconscious brain and how to exert control over its vast potential to control our lives. —Sam Lottel

Packed full of insights to changing bad money habits, this book is well written and highly recommended. — Ed Jensen

Thank you for this book. It is a well-researched and effective way to change old money habits. This book should be required reading in every school. —Clint Cardoza

Contents

Introduction		7
Chapter 1	Wealth	11
	Money consciousness	11
	Your right to wealth	14
	Paper or Plastic	22
	Borrowing money	24
	Thought precedes form	30
	Life seeks increase	34
	Live below your means	38
Chapter 2	Greed	43
	Hoarding	47
	Poverty and wealth	48
	Prosperity	51
	Poverty	54
	Negative money beliefs	56
	Wealth Consciousness	66
Chapter 3	Gambling Addiction	69
	Gambling habit change	77
Chapter 4	Habit Change	83
	How Habits Work	87
	Cue, Action, Reward	89
	Beliefs	98
	Summary of Chapter	102
Chapter 5	Subconscious Control	105
	Subconscious Mind	110
	Conscious Mind	122
	Control Subconscious	125
	PREP	127
	SSSS	134
	Summary of the Chapter	149
Conclusion		155
About the Author		157

Introduction

Congratulations on your decision to control your financial life. If your are motivated to become rich, only your old ways of thinking about money can can keep you from achieving your goals.

It's amazing how many people blame society or someone else for the problems in their lives. They blame their lots in life on upbringing, family, health, bad luck, lack of money, or 'the man' (usually the government or their boss).

You will learn in this book that the external world does exert some influence over your habit formation, but you can regain control any time you choose. In fact, the blame game is the thing that gives you the illusion that you have less power than you really have. You can continue to blame someone else, or you can learn to take responsibility for your financial situations and learn how to change them. Your life can be so much easier than you imagine.

When people discover that they that they are faced with money problems, they sometimes lose their self-respect and replace it with self-disgust or even self-loathing. When they finally learn to manage their money over the long term, they often feel they are finally a success and their real lives have finally begun. Money gives us opportunities, control, and the extra time to do what we want with our life.

Major change of any kind is often fearful. For

many people with money issues, the mere thought of changing their long-held beliefs about money can fill them with fear. You may have a goal of one day having enough money, but today may not be the day. You may have previously tried to take charge of your finances, but after much hard work and effort failed. Taking control of your money is a combination of simple math and the desire to do it. But keeping long term control of your money requires you to regain control of your habits.

The most important thing in achieving financial freedom is to make habits your friends and allies instead of your enemies and destroyers. Changing an undesirable money habit can be very difficult if you do not understand how to do it. This is because your habits are implanted very deep within your subconscious mind. Trying to fight or resist a bad habit without knowing how often just gives strength to the habit itself. The key to changing habits is to use the methods of habit change and subconscious mind control that you will find in the last two chapters of this book.

The *Conquer and Control* method is real. It is different than anything you have tried before. If you truly want to regain control of your financial life, this method will work. You can be in the driver's seat instead of the passenger seat of your life.

It doesn't matter if you had poor grades or how far you got school. This method of regaining control your finances works because it combines the latest knowledge on habit change with state of the art technology on subconscious mind control. Taken together, you will have the tools you need to take your life back. There is no other book like this one.

Chapter one gives you you basic information about about wealth. It addresses the problems that an unhealthy money consciousness can cause and provides you with the basics of how to approach those problems.

Chapter two addresses both greed and hoarding. It also speaks about prosperity and wealth and how you can change your money consciousness.

Chapter three talks about gambling addiction and how it can destroy your financial well being.

Chapter four explains how habits work. Once you understand the makeup of your life-destroying habits, you can determine which part(s) of the habit to change.

Chapter five teaches you that financial success must begin in your mind. The most important factor to financial success is to have both your conscious mind and subconscious mind in clear agreement of your goal. Only with your conscious and subconscious in complete agreement will you be able to focus all your mental energy on the attainment of the goal. Then your subconscious mind will work steadfastly, even when you are asleep, towards attaining your goal.

That chapter also gives you the tools you need to use your conscious mind to reprogram your subconscious mind. You will use this reprogramming to change the habit parts you select from chapter four.

Together, the five chapters of this book give you everything you need to change any negative money habits that could be holding you back.

A good life requires enough control of your mind to adjust the factors that can lead to positive financial changes in your life. That is what this book is about.

> You are always free to change your mind and choose a different future, or a different past. — Richard Bach

Chapter One

Wealth

MONEY CONSCIOUSNESS

Early in life when you were still a small child, you began to acquire your money consciousness. You listened to and observed your parents or whoever else was around. And for better or worse, you picked up many of their money beliefs. You may have acquired useful and positive beliefs about money, or possibly a poverty consciousness.

These early beliefs and opinions went directly into your subconscious mind with little filtering from your developing brain. This early misinformation can remain with you for your whole life. Even today, the way you react to money may be influenced by those early inner beliefs that stay in your subconscious mind. Unfortunately, poorer parents hand down their limiting money beliefs to their children, and wealthier parents hand down their unlimited money beliefs to their children.

These early beliefs can cause either positive or negative thoughts and emotions about the subject of money. Unless you consciously decide to change these thoughts, they will remain with you for your entire life.

These thoughts can color your perceptions so that you may actually believe that poverty is good or that you do not deserve to be wealthy. But the fact is that wealth is good and you do deserve to be rich.

Still, many people are terrified of money and wealth. On one hand, they want to be rich, but on the other hand they believe that they will have to work too hard, that it is not spiritual, or that it's just plain evil and wrong. Other misconceptions are that wealth means greed or dishonesty, or taking advantage of others. Then there is the false belief that money is a zero sum game. Even though America is richer than ever before in history, the false belief still exists that to make money you must take it away from someone else. Still other false beliefs are that money cannot buy happiness, money makes you neglect your family, and that there are no opportunities left to make a lot of money.

These and similar misconceptions are not necessarily true but may have found a home deep down in your subconscious mind. These beliefs about money are now taken as real. Usually, you do not even examine them. They are just accepted. They may have given you a low financial self-worth: a poverty consciousness. They may make you resent wealthy people and reject the idea of ever being rich yourself.

> Very few people can afford to be poor.
> — George Bernard Shaw

Chapter One Wealth

One example of where these beliefs come from is someone who was raised in a family that argued and had a lot of anger about money. As a child the take away was money causes fighting and anger. Now as an adult their subconscious mind associates money and anger.

If this person starts to make a lot of money, they may feel an increase in their anger. They are uncomfortable with this anger, so they sabotage their new money making ability. They can do this without even knowing why. It comes from a deep subconscious negative association of money. This book will assist in reprogramming your subconscious for wealth instead of poverty.

> As much money and life as you could want! The two things most human beings would choose above all - the trouble is, humans do have a knack of choosing precisely those things that are worst for them. — J. K. Rowling

If you are unhappy with your financial condition, just look at the cause. And the cause is the way your mind was taught to think about money. Your beliefs about money no longer serve you. They obstruct your efforts to become rich.

In order to change your financial conditions you must first change the way you think about money. Trying to change only your external conditions will not work. This book will assist you to improve your thoughts and beliefs about money.

It is not important what your past or present

situations are. It is not important how many times you have previously failed in financial matters. This book will show you how to have a prosperity consciousness. It will show you how to increase your wealth and success.

> A lack of money is not the problem; it's merely a symptom of what's going on inside you. — T. Harvey Eker

YOUR RIGHT TO WEALTH

It is much easier to attain happiness and personal development if you have enough money. Very few people can rise to their highest development unless they have money to buy things to use.

Everyone has a right to all the growth and development they are capable of attaining. Since people develop by making use of things, they must have enough money to buy these things.

Everyone's right to life, liberty, and the pursuit of happiness means they must make it their business to have the things that are necessary to their spiritual, mental, and physical growth; or, in other words, their right to be wealthy.

> Money is like a sixth sense without which you cannot make a complete use of the other five. — W. Somerset Maugham

Most people naturally want to become all

that they are capable of becoming. This desire is inherent in human nature. Success in life is becoming what you want to be. You can become what you want to be only by making use of things, and you can have the use of things only as you become rich enough to buy them. So there is nothing wrong in wanting to be wealthy.

The desire for wealth is really the desire to attain your dreams and ambitions. It is through the use of material things that a person finds full life for his body, develops his mind, and unfolds his soul. It is therefore of the most importance to each individual to be wealthy.

> Poverty is a great enemy to human happiness. It certainly destroys liberty, and it makes some virtues impractical, and others extremely difficult.
> — Samuel Johnson

It is entirely proper that you should desire to be wealthy. If you are a normal person you cannot help doing so. It is perfectly right that you put forth your best efforts to becoming wealthy so that you can make the most of yourself.

YOU CAN BECOME WEALTHY

Becoming wealthy is not a matter of where you live or in choosing a particular business or profession. When two people are in the same city and in the same business, and one gets rich while the other remains poor, it shows that wealth is not primarily a matter of location. Some locations may be more favorable than others, but when two people in the same business are in the same neighborhood and one gets rich while the other fails, it indicates that becoming wealthy is the result of something more.

Becoming wealthy does not depend on formal education, even advanced degrees in business and accounting. I have a relative who has an MBA earning over $100,000 a year but is poor. He spends more than he makes and his credit cards are all maxed out. He lives paycheck to paycheck and juggles which bills to pay. Many self-made millionaires do not have any collage degrees.

The ability to become wealthy is not due solely to the possession of talent, for many people who have great talent remain poor, while others who have very little talent get rich.

Studying the people who became wealthy, we find that they are an average lot in all respects, having no greater talents and abilities than other people have. Evidently they do not get rich because they possess more talents and abilities then others. Nor is getting rich due to doing things that others fail to do. Two people in the same business often do almost exactly the same things, and one gets rich while the other goes bankrupt. From all these things, we must come to the conclusion that getting rich is the result of understanding and using the principles of wealth.

Talented people get rich, and untalented people get rich; collage graduates get rich, and

Chapter One Wealth

uneducated people get rich. Some degree of ability to think and understand is, of course, essential. But insofar as natural ability is concerned, any person who has sense enough to read and understand these words can certainly become wealthy.

There is a story about a man who ordered an expensive suit from Zumbach the tailor. When the time came to try on the suit the man complained that one sleeve was too long. Zumbach the tailor said that nothing was wrong with the suit, but the man's stance was bad so he had the man bend to one side. Sure enough, the sleeve was now the right length.

Then the man noticed that there was material bunched up at the back of his neck and told Zumbach. "It's not the suit, it's the way you're standing", replied Zumbach and had the man bend forward.

So finally the suit fits right and the man walks out of Zumbach's shop. But now the man's body is contorted and he looks like a cripple, but the suit looks good.

The same type of thing happens when you try to conform yourself to a job that may look good, but cripples your motivation and enthusiasm. You try to conform to a concept that you do not believe and your energy is contorted and rendered useless.

No one knows your passion and purpose better than you. You must decide whether you can work in your present job or a complete change is necessary. You must decide if it feels right for you to put your whole effort behind your current job or if something else will serve you better.

It is not a matter of choosing some particular business or profession because you have heard that you can make a lot of money in it. Computer programming and starting dot com companies may be lucrative, but if you have no computer skills or don't like that type of business, you will not do well. You will do best in a business that you like and which is congenial to you. If you have certain talents that are well developed, you will do best in a business that calls for the exercise of those talents. Also, you will do best in a business that is suited to your locality.

> Most successful men have not achieved their distinction by having some new talent or opportunity presented to them. They have developed the opportunity that was at hand. — Bruce Marton

You may have been told that it takes money to make money. But no one is prevented from becoming rich by lack of capital. True, as you get capital the increase becomes easier and more rapid. No matter how poor you may be, if you begin to understand and use the principles of wealth you will begin to get rich and you will begin to have capital. Getting capital is a part of the process of getting rich and it is a part of the result that invariably follows.

You may be the poorest person in the world and be deeply in debt. You may have neither friends, influence, nor resources, but if you understand and use the principles of wealth, you will begin to get rich.

Today, in America, we live in the most prosperous society in the history of the world. There is a surplus of food, shelter, and money. There is an abundance of opportunity for any person who seeks it. No one is held in poverty by a scarcity in the supply of riches. There is more than enough for all.

The Internet and World Wide Web are perfect examples of huge wealth opportunities that came from the invisible supply. The ascent of information technology is changing our lives at unparalleled speeds. A few-hundred-dollar investment in your own Internet business can still create vast wealth. The Internet bubble that burst mainly affected stock gamblers, but revenue from the Internet still continues to make annual double digit increases.

And there continue to be more and more opportunities. Three-dimension printing will eventually change many types of manufacturing. And we are still in the infancy of that evolution. Nano technology will also change many products and already has change some. I could go on and on about the revolutionary developments all around us. There is no doubt that the opportunities are here now.

The best way to create money is to become involve in a business or venture that you enjoy. It is even better if that business is one where you have proper skills or where you can acquire those skills.

Take some time to determine your skills and

your desires. Make a plan and write it down so that you know which direction you choose to move. A plan is a clear and concise map that will take you from where you are to where you want to be. Include deadlines when you want to attain certain results. A plan keeps you on purpose in your daily activities. In the future, if there is a good reason, you can always revise this plan. You need a plan both to stay on purpose and to visualize during the exercises in the subconscious mind chapter of this book.

> The secret of success is constancy of purpose. — Benjamin Disraeli

If you are just starting out, it is usually a good idea to work for a business similar to the one in your plan. That way you will learn how business operates and acquire skills in that business. You may chose to remain in that business and work your way up or you may eventually start your own business with similar but newer and better ideas.

> The creation of a thousand forests is in one acorn. — Ralph Waldo Emerson

The visible supply is practically inexhaustible, and the invisible supply really is inexhaustible. All the houses and cars and everything you see come from one original substance, out of which all things proceed. New forms are constantly being made, and older ones are dissolving. There is no limit to the supply of formless stuff, or original substance. Ten thousand times as much as has been made might still be made, and even then we will not exhaust the supply of universal raw material.

A few hundred years ago, alchemists experimented with ways to turn base metal into gold. They never succeeded but today we can do even better. Today there is no limit to the wealth available to us.

Intel Corporation is an example of a company that takes sand (silicon) and turns it into computer chips that, pound for pound, are worth more than gold. Just regular sand is manipulated with ideas to accomplish this feat. This process uses heat, masking, and doping to accomplish this alchemy. It almost sounds illegal but it's just another example of wealth created from almost worthless raw ingredients. As of this writing the most powerful IBM computer chip is named "True North" and it has only about 5.4 billion transistors and compares in capability to the brain of an insect. But it opens up many additional opportunities for entrepreneurs who can learn skills in these areas.

> All wealth begins in the mind.
> — Napoleon Hill

No one is poor because nature is poor or because there is not enough to go around. Nature is an inexhaustible storehouse of riches; the supply will never run short. Nature is alive with creative energy, and is constantly producing more forms. When the supply of building material is exhausted, more will be produced. Homes may be made of plastic, metal, concrete, or some new material, and the potentials are infinite.

> All the breaks you need in life wait within your imagination.
> — Napoleon Hill

You are not kept poor by lack in the supply of riches. There are absolutely huge amounts of money circulating in our economy. You are kept poor only by your lack of understanding of the principles of wealth.

PAPER OR PLASTIC?

In today's world, money is a major moving force in our lives. In fact, money can be thought of as a form of energy. Most people do not really understand money. But we must understand and come to terms with money if we are to live a successful life.

Early exchanges used barter and trading. At that time it was easy to see what buying a chicken was worth in terms of work. Then came the first disconnect with the arrival of gold, silver and copper, which were soon fashioned into coins. Now a chicken was worth a certain coin.

Paper came next and it separated us more from the real value of that chicken. At first it was backed by gold and silver but that connection was eventually removed. Now our government just prints money and we have the illusion of currency. Then plastic took over. Now you just swipe a credit card and the chicken is yours. Hundreds of miles away, some computer has changed the value of that chicken into a string of ones and zeros. Even plastic is evolving; now your smart phone can transfer your money for you. Most people still cannot believe that their name and all their money are just ones and zeros in some distant computer. It seems like an illusion and that it's very far removed from reality.

> All money is a matter of belief.
> — Adam Smith

Speaking of ones and zeros, many fortunes have been created by them. It's exactly like creating wealth out of nothing. One example is the software company Microsoft that has created thousands of millionaires as well as some billionaires from those ones and zeros.

In the early 80s, Bill Gates saw an Apple Macintosh computer and knew that he needed to appropriate this concept and replace the difficult MS-DOS operating system with Windows. It was just a matter of manipulating some ones and zeros to get this much more user-friendly windows interface. The problem occurred when Apple filed the WIMP lawsuit (**W**indows, **I**con, **M**ouse, **P**ointer) to keep Gates from using their windows interface.

Well Microsoft eventually won the lawsuit

because it was shown that Apple itself had appropriated this innovation from the Palo Alto Research Center (PARC), a subsidiary of Xerox Corporation. So it turns out that most of this enormous Microsoft wealth and the Apple wealth came from someone else's ideas that were turned into ones and zeros that exist as invisible electrons inside a computer. Wealth was indeed created from nothing. In fact, in the last 50 years, more wealth has been created than in the all the previous years put together.

The entire world is changing more quickly today than ever before. Technology, ways of going to market, product cycles, outsourcing, and styles are all changing. Today there are more fertile fields where people can make millions than ever before in history. This continually opens huge opportunities for people to make enormous amounts of money. Increasing your wealth has never been so easy.

BORROWING MONEY IS GOOD AND BAD.

So here we are in a world where the money is not real any more and you can get one or a hundred chickens with that same swipe of plastic. It's no wonder that so many people have lost touch with reality and, on average, owe many thousands of dollars to their credit card companies. The interest rates credit card companies charge are unbelievable. At those rates it becomes very difficult to ever pay off your card.

> Having money is a way of being free of money. — Albert Camus

There are two kinds of loans. The first is consumer loans where you spend the money you borrow to buy things for your own use. This is a bad loan since in the long run it ends up costing much more than you borrowed. Buying on time often means paying twice as much as buying with cash. And you are often spending money on things that you do not even want or need.

This money is usually spent out of a subconscious habit during your walk through the shopping mall. Buying excessively may temporally make you feel good, but it is a drug, and the bill that comes next month is the hangover. Buying on credit is an expensive habit and will hurt you on your path to wealth.

Even millionaires can be caught up in overspending and before long end up penniless; and worse, often with millions in debt. Stop borrowing money to spend on unnecessary consumables. Do not use your credit card if you do not pay it off in full every single month.

Be frugal with your resources. If you can't afford to pay cash for a new car, buy an older model where you do not have to take out a loan. Do not throw your money away, but use it for your advancement. Wasting the wealth that comes to you shows a lack of gratitude for that money. Even though you have unlimited supply, you must still respect and be grateful for your abundance.

It is normal to enjoy the marvelous experiences and things wealth can bring us. There is nothing wrong with using your money in this manor. Still, you must remember that it is the uncontrolled desire for these things that puts many people in financial difficulty. Your road to wealth must be balanced. You must be frugal when you need to, but free and easy in your spending when you can afford it. Frugal does not mean being a cheap scrooge as depicted in Dickens's *Christmas Carol* book. It is important to spend some money on play, vacations, and entertainment. This is a positive reinforcement for increasing your wealth. Your subconscious mind will get this message and work harder to increase you wealth still further.

> Definition of frugal – economy in the expenditure of resources. Frugal comes from the Latin word frug which means virtue; a commendable quality or trait.

The second kind of loan is a business loan where you use other people's money to make more money. This is often good since it is a way to increase your wealth. Many fortunes were made using other people's money.

Business and real estate would be far more difficult if not for our ability to borrow money. Borrowing money can leverage a piece of property. In some cases, you need to put nothing or relatively little down so you have tremendous leverage. If you increase the value of the property you could make a profit of well over one hundred percent.

> When you borrow money, you should always think how you're going to pay it back. — Dmitry Medvedev

You should save ten percent of your money. This means take that ten percent of your take home pay and put it in separate bank or stock account before you spend anything else. Even if your take home pay is very small, save that magical ten percent. Your subconscious mind relates to the number ten because we have ten fingers. Consequently, our number system is based on ten. Even the old Roman number system was based on ten.

This ten percent by itself will not create wealth, but this practice is a discipline that will provide your seed money and send the subconscious energy of wealth your way.

Everyone has expenses that they can cut to put that ten percent in the bank. Now, this ten percent will start the energy of wealth coming your way. This is not to be used to buy things. Instead, it should be invested in appreciable assets so that it will increase in value. And I do not mean investing in risky stocks that are no better than gambling, or marketing gimmicks dressed up as investments. Begin with investments in a few diversified exchange traded funds (ETF) that charges minimal fees.

Don't try to time the market because even experts have difficulty doing this. And don't pay someone to actively manage your account since this often means frequent stock trading that depletes you money in fees and commissions.

Invest for the long haul or use your savings to start a business or rental real estate that you have very thoroughly investigated. If you don't know of such a business, continue to save that ten percent of your money until you do know. But avoid major risks.

The number one rule in investing is don't lose your money. This requires that you don't put all your eggs in one basket. Be diversified so that if one investment goes bad your others will stay strong. This means that in addition to American stocks of various types, you need foreign stocks and other appreciating investments.

> I tell people investing should be dull. It shouldn't be exciting. Investing should be more like watching paint dry or watching grass grow. If you want excitement, take $800 and go to Las Vegas. — Paul Samuelson, Nobel Laureate in Economics

Some people are so deeply in debt that there is no way they could reasonably repay their loans. They should consider credit consolidation, but that may still carry too large a financial burden. The constant letters and phone calls from collection agencies make it very difficult to retain a prosperity consciousness. For these people, it is better that they acknowledge this and declare bankruptcy. Knowing this, our government created bankruptcy laws so that people can start over. Evoking this law can create understandable anxiety. People ask about destroying their credit and losing credit cards.

> I don't measure a man's success by how high he climbs but how high he bounces when he hits bottom.
> — General George Patton

As strange as it sounds, bankruptcy can sometimes improve bad credit. Your credit rating may be so low that if you have a good income, your rating could go up. This is because you can only declare it once every eight years. So lenders know that now you cannot declare another chapter seven bankrupt for eight more years and if you don't pay they can garnish your wages. You will be able to find high-risk credit cards where you put up a certain amount of money at the bank to guarantee payment.

> If you can dream it, you can do it.
> — Walt Disney

Abraham Lincoln, Mark Twain, Henry Ford, and Walt Disney are a few of the many famous people who had to declare bankruptcy before they could go on to their success. You are entitled to make a mistake and start over. That is why the laws are there. But now you must take responsibility and not let this happen again. Now you must save that magic 10 percent of your income and go on to create millions.

> If you would be wealthy, think of saving as well as getting. — Benjamin Franklin

You also need to stop that needless shopping and use that money to save that magical 10%. While you are doing that, you should also be reading and working on the rest of this book. But it is important to know that you can make it on what you now have. The starting point for wealth is to be thankful for what you have now and to have a vision of what you want next.

THOUGHT PRECEDES FORM

We live in a thought world. Thoughts have no mass and are invisible, but they can cause the creation of the forms that we do see. The thought of a house of a particular size and construction could cause workers to build that house. Or perhaps a house meeting your requirements could go on sale and you were following the real estate listings. It all starts with an invisible thought.

It is the same in nature. We can just look and see the abundance and quality of the apples on a tree. But the apples really start below ground where we do not look. It is the invisible roots of the apple tree that collect the nutrition that creates those big apples. If the roots are inadequate, the abundance of the apples will suffer. If we fertilize and care for the invisible roots, the harvest will be abundant.

As humans we are all capable of enormous quantities of original thought. All the forms that people shape with their hands and tools must first exist in thoughts. A person cannot shape a thing until after the thought of that thing. A person can form things in thought, and can cause the thing to be physically created.

> All riches have their origin in mind.
> Wealth is in ideas, not money.
> — Robert Collier

People get rich by understanding and using the principles of wealth. A person's way of doing things is the direct result of the way that person thinks about things. To do things in the way you want to do them, you will have to acquire the ability to think the way you want to think. This is the first step toward becoming wealthy. Think what you want to think regardless of outward appearances.

Individuals have the natural and inherent power to think their own thoughts. But it requires far more effort to do so than it does to think the thoughts suggested by appearances. To think according to appearances is easy. To think your own truth regardless of appearances is difficult. It requires the expenditure of quite a bit of willpower. It is not easy to look at a beach full of silicone sand and see a computer chip.

> Your thoughts are the tools with which you carve your life story on the substance of our universe. When you choose your thoughts, you choose results. — Imelda Shanklin

When the Wright Brothers set out to build an airplane, most people said they were crazy and said that it could not be done. But the Wright Brothers held firm to their thoughts in spite of appearances. Their thoughts created an airplane, and today we can fly faster than the speed of sound and have landed men on the moon.

> It takes courage to do what you want. Other people have a lot of plans for you. — Joseph Campbell

Sustained thought is some of the hardest work in the world. This is especially true when thoughts are conflicting with appearances, and when everyone else tells you that it cannot be done.

Every appearance in the visible world tends to produce a corresponding form in the mind that observes it. To look upon the appearances of poverty will produce corresponding forms in your own mind. You create your own wealth, and you create your own poverty. That is why it is necessary to hold on to the thought that there is no poverty; there is only abundance. To think riches when in the midst of the appearances of poverty requires power. But whoever acquires this power is set free from the appearance of poverty. These people can conquer fate and can have whatever they want.

> Men who accomplish great things in the industrial world are the ones who have faith in the money producing power of ideas. — Charles Fillmore

This power can only be acquired by getting hold of the fact that is behind all appearances. That fact is that thoughts are more powerful than form. We must understand the truth that every thought can become a form. We can impress these thoughts upon our subconscious mind to cause the thoughts to take form and become visible things.

When we finally realize this truth, we lose all doubt and fear. We know that we can create what we want to create. We can have what we want to have. We can become what we want to be.

> Man was born to be rich, or grows rich by the use of his faculties, by the union of thought with nature.
> — Ralph Waldo Emerson

As a first step toward getting wealth, you should accept that a person can form things in their thoughts, and this can cause the thing they think about to be created. You should put aside all other concepts of the universe and dwell upon this until you fix it in your mind and it has become your habitual thought. If a doubt comes to you, cast it aside. Do not be persuaded by arguments against this idea.

When you accept the power of your thought, everything changes. It is phenomenal. The entire world seems to change with your new reality. Wealth begins with the acceptance of the power of your thought and your intentions.

> Keep away from people who try to belittle your ambitions. Small people always do that, but the really great make you feel that you, too, are great.
> — Mark Twain

LIFE SEEKS INCREASE

Do not believe for even a second that poverty will bring you closer to God or that rich people cannot go to heaven. That is misinformation invented by those in poverty to make their condition seem less shameful. A simple observation of evolution and nature shows that life must continually seek expansion. It always has and it always will.

All life, in the mere act of living, must increase itself. A seed, dropped into the ground, springs into activity, and in the act of living produces hundreds more seeds. A few humans began their existence only about 200,000 years ago. And now there are over seven billion humans on the earth. Life is forever becoming more. It has no choice, and must do so for it to continue to be life.

> Money isn't everything, but lack of money isn't anything.
> — Franklin Adams

Intelligence falls under this same principle of necessity for continuous increase. Every thought we think makes it necessary for us to think another thought; consciousness is continually expanding. Every fact we learn leads us to learn another fact. Knowledge is continually increasing. We have invented smart phones and ask Siri questions and it responds with the facts. Every talent we cultivate brings to our mind the desire to cultivate another talent. We are subject to the urge of life to increase and expand. It drives us on to know more, to do more, and to be more. And soon we will learn to enlist the power of our subconscious mind.

In order to know more, do more, and be more, we must have more. The desire for wealth is simply the desire of life seeking fulfillment. Every desire is the effort of an unexpressed possibility to come into existence. It is the power of life seeking to manifest itself in form. That which makes you want more money is the same as that which makes plants grow and propagate. It is life seeking a fuller expression of life. Every living thing is subject to this inherent law of increase. It is infused with the desire to live more, and that is why life has the need to multiply and create a larger life.

Increase is nature's universal plan. It desires

36 Conquer and Control

you to have everything you want to have. Nature is friendly to your plans. Wealth accumulation is much easier if you can accept that this is true.

It is essential, however, that your purpose should harmonize with growth and life. You want to get rich in order that you may eat, drink, and be merry when it is time to do these things. You want to get rich in order that you may surround yourself with beautiful things, see distant lands, feed your mind, and develop your intellect. You want to get rich in order that you may love others and do kind deeds, and be able to play a good part in helping the world to improve. You can make the most of yourself by getting rich, so it is right that you should give your thoughts to the work of acquiring wealth.

> Lack of money is the root of all evil.
> — George Bernard Shaw

Do not think of getting rich by taking things away from someone else. Money is not a zero sum game. You do not have to take your wealth from others. You are to create more, not to fight for what is already created. You do not have to take anything away from anyone. You do not have to cheat or lie or take advantage of others. You do not need to have anyone work for you for substandard wages.

You do not have to fight for the property of others. No one has anything that you cannot duplicate. You are to become a creator, not a fighter. You are going to get what you want, but in such a way that when you get it every other person who you do business with will have more than they have now. All your negotiations and trades with others will be win-win.

There are those who get wealth by stealing, fighting and lying. But most people who get rich in this way end up with unhappy and miserable lives. Riches secured in this way are never satisfactory and permanent. They are yours today and gone tomorrow.

> One of the greatest discoveries a man makes, one of his greatest surprises, is to find he can do what he was afraid he couldn't do. — Henry Ford

You must always remember that the supply of money is unlimited. Do not think that all the money is being cornered and controlled by others, and that you must exert yourself to get laws passed to stop this process. Instead of win-lose thinking, replace it with win-win thinking. Never look only at the visible supply. Look also at the limitless riches in the invisible supply, and know that these riches will come to you.

> There are always opportunities through which businessmen can profit handsomely if they will only recognize and seize them.
> — J. Paul Getty

Nobody, by cornering the visible supply, can prevent you from getting what is yours. So never allow yourself to think that, unless you hurry, all the best building spots will be taken before you get ready to build your house. Never worry about the mega corporations and get anxious for fear they will soon come to own the whole earth. Never be afraid that you will lose what you want because some other person beats you to it. Never be afraid that all jobs will move to India or China. You are causing creation from formless substance, and that supply is without limits.

No one can limit your supply. There are no limits to your journey to grow and experience life. You will discover all that you want to be or do or have in life will be yours. But stay focused, allow sufficient time, question everything and do no be distracted by the opinions of so-called authorities.

Remember in 1615, it was the authorities that convicted Galilei Galileo of heresy for saying the earth traveled around the sun when science already proved that the sun travels around the earth. Everyone knew that earth was the center of the universe and Galileo was a denier of that fact. So much for authorities.

Live below your means

> The art of living easy is to pitch your scale of living one degree below your means. — Sir Henry Taylor

Buying depreciable assets like the huge homes, the latest smart phone, boats and planes is spending (wasting) money and will decrease your wealth. Spending more money than you have on consumables disobeys the prime rules of money creation. It squanders your resources and usually leads to bad credit and financial hardship. Eventually, it can result in poverty.

On the other hand, buying capital assets such as quality stocks or starting your own business is investing and will increase your net worth. It is not enough to stop wasting money and focus on saving it. Instead you should not continue wasting money and in its place invest it.

I don't mean investing it at the gambling casino where the odds are way against you. I am talking about investing it in your own business or less risky assets that give you modest gains but that compound annually.

One of the best ways to invest is to build a business of your own. Remember that money is an inner mind to outer reality concept. Your business comes from within you. You may have been considering it for years, but suddenly it all comes together in your mind. It may be a totally new business or a new spin on an existing business model. Whatever it is, this is your path to money.

It takes courage to create your own business and you might fail. As I said earlier, many famous people have failed in various endeavors. You may fail once, twice, or three times, but if you follow the directions in this book you will eventually succeed.

> The failures of President Abraham Lincoln, a man who would not give up:
> At age twenty-two he failed in business.
> At age twenty-three he lost the election for the state legislature.
> At age twenty-four he failed in business for the second time.
> At age twenty-six his beloved fiancée died.
> At age twenty-seven he suffered a nervous breakdown.
> At age thirty-four he lost the election for a House seat.
> At age thirty-seven he was elected to to the House.
> At age thirty-nine he lost the election for a House seat again.
> At age forty-six he lost the election for a Senate seat.
> At age forty-seven he lost the election for vice-president.
> At age forty-nine he lost the election for a Senate seat yet again.
> Finally at age fifty-one he was elected president of United States.

It's not how much money you have or keep that is the important issue. It is how and why you spend it. Or invest it. Or blow it.

My definition of a wealthy person is someone who makes more than they spend and puts the difference is an account that will give them another stream of money. Many people who make hundreds of thousands of dollars a year have to juggle their finances to pay off their monthly credit cards. These people are poor.

So it's not how much money you make today that makes you rich. It is how much you keep and invest in an even richer tomorrow.

Millions of hardworking men and women toil away at their jobs, giving 100 percent dedication and commitment, only to come home every day exhausted and with no other option but to return to the treadmill the next day. When it comes to your career, you can make only as much money as there are hours in the day. But if you invest some of your money, it won't be long before you can think of getting off the treadmill and having a real and joyful life.

Your time on earth is limited; so don't waste it worrying about not having enough money to do what you want. Don't waste it getting on that treadmill every day. Have the courage to change your money consciousness and open up a whole new world for your enjoyment.

Chapter Two
Greed

Life is like a pendulum that swings back and forth. When it moves too far in one direction the forces of nature cause it to reverse and move in the other direction. It is the same with money.

Sometimes when a person swings from a poverty consciousness to a money consciousness they can go too far. They learn to acquire a lot of money but they forget that the purpose of money is to enhance their life. If they just hoard their money without using it for betterment they are no better off then when they were poor. If they become greedy or miserly they will not get the full benefits of the money they earned.

The advice for these people will often be the opposite of the advice given to those who have no money. Instead of not spending but instead saving, the overly frugal person needs to spend more of their money and save less. This chapter will address greed as well as wealth consciousness.

> The difference between greed and ambition is a greedy person desires things he isn't prepared to work for.
> — Habeeb Akande

The greedy person is stingy, hoards things, and never has enough. This causes intense unhappiness. The greed could be for money, possessions, power, gain, fame, approval, experiences, status, knowledge, information, or really just about anything. The greedy person often desires things only for the sake of possessing them rather than for the benefit of the items themselves.

Greed often stems from fear of lack or deprivation of things. This fear creates a need to have more than enough so one will never run out. Greed is a taking and hoarding, much like the "pack rat" that takes things it does not need. The problem is that greed stands in opposition to our enjoying the things in life instead of just owning and storing them. It was insatiable greed that killed the goose who laid the golden eggs.

Money and possessions can be addictive, similar to a drug. When we begin to sacrifice our other aspirations to the pursuit of getting these possessions, we know we are addicted. And just like other addictions, the instructions in this book will free you.

A large portion of the wrongs and crimes of history has been due to the inordinate greed for money. Greed is about more than just wanting more money or material possessions. Greed is the desire to possess more than is useful. It is the need to have much more so than we never run out.

Many people want to make a certain amount of money but, after their goal is met, do not stop. They want to make more and more money.

These people believe that if they make a million dollars they will be satisfied and happy for the rest of their lives. However, if they do make that million dollars, it doesn't take long before a second and then a third million dollars are desired. It becomes a never-ending pursuit to accumulate more. Ultimately, the money brings no lasting happiness or satisfaction. It's no wonder that the word 'miser' was chosen to identify someone who is miserable.

Greed doesn't just encompass money. Greed can be about accumulating too much power, or knowledge or even compulsive collections of any thing.

An example of the greed associated with the desire for more information is someone who accumulates a vast storehouse of knowledge and will not share it with others. It's the hoarding without sharing that presents a problem. The characteristic that all types of greed have in common is that they stem from a deep fear of life and produce pointless desires that do not result in the greedy person's happiness.

Greed can become so overwhelming that it becomes the primary purpose of life. Greed is harmful to the well-being of society, but more importantly, it will have a fatal effect upon your life because your energy is wasted in accumulating some thing instead of seeking to enjoy life and grow as a person.

The myth of King Midas relates the story of how greed caused the King to wish for the power to turn everything he touched into gold. He was granted this wish and, to test it, he put his finger upon a bowl of fruit. It was instantly transmuted into pure gold. He excitedly turned numerous other objects into gold.

In the excitement of the miracle, he absent-mindedly took his young daughter by the hand to lead her into the garden. King Midas was horrified to find that she had turned into a life-size golden statue with no sign of life.

From that point on, he couldn't touch any useful object without it losing its utility. Because of the King's greed, even his food turned into gold, losing all its value as a food.

Another indication of greed is when a person lives beyond their monetary means. Many people frequent shopping malls where almost all the products they buy are luxuries and not necessary for their life. They "shop till they drop," and this often results in credit card problems and difficulty paying many bills. We have built an affluent economy on the production of things that people do not really need. Through advertising, we create a need for these items. In the free world, there are relatively few people who live below the poverty line. Therefore, this overspending occurs not to meet normal basic needs, but to buy more of the things that a greedy person desires. One bumper sticker that was popular a few years ago proclaimed, "Born to shop."

> Hell has three gates: lust, anger and greed. — Bhagavad Gita (Hindu Bible)

When a man has a large amount of wealth,

we call him "a man of means." Not infrequently, the phrase is a misnomer. This is because the 'means' imply the 'ends' to which they are devoted, and many a wealthy man has no such ends. He does not know why he makes money. He is like a hamster running on an exercise wheel, accustomed to the monotonous round and round motion. He is the slave of the money or possessions, which claim all his thoughts and all his energy. Yet, the phrase, "a man of means" conveys the message that money can be used in promoting rational and useful ends, and this is true. People often speculate on what good things they would do with money if they had an immense amount of it. But the speculations are mere illusions unless they control the money and possessions rather than the reverse being true.

Hoarding

Hoarding is a subset of greed and is collecting things to excess. This does not mean the approximately forty percent of Americans who, as a hobby, collect things like stamps, guns, miniatures dolls, coins, and thousands of other items. Hoarding is way beyond normal collecting and could be called eccentricity or even pathology. Some psychologists claim that this stems from a subconscious desire to leave something after our death and in that way have some claim on immortality. Others say that it is about believing that we are the material objects that we own. Whatever the reason, hoarding has the potential to destroy our lives.

Hoarding has financially destroyed some people, leaving them without enough funds to even feed themselves. Others frequent garage sales, go dumpster diving, or even steal. But they still end up with out of control homes filled with things that clutter and take over their lives. Consequently, they lose the freedom that a more organized home can give them.

POVERTY AND WEALTH

> You can have anything you want if you will give up the belief that you can't have it. — Robert Anthony

To be in poverty is defined as lacking the usual or socially acceptable amount of money or material possessions. By definition, the average person in poverty today has much more than many middle class people just a hundred years ago. Back then you had to be rich to have a car and there was no possibility of having a cell phone or television. Today almost everyone in the poverty class has these things and much more. This does not mean that poverty is what we should settle for in life, but at least it is not starting from zero. So now it is even easier than it used to be to become rich.

Of course in modern America, a family of four who knows how to play the various government programs can receive about three thousand dollars a month in welfare checks. Additionally, there are many other free items such as food stamp credit cards, free cell phones, et cetera. Often off-the-book employment such as odd jobs or even working at a meth lab augment the government money. The real problem here is that the family's subconscious poverty mentality is continually reinforced by the welfare and thus lessening the odds that they will ever learn how to set themselves free.

In 1964, President Johnson declared a war on poverty. Today, after more than fifty years and untold trillions of dollars wasted, the percent of people in poverty is basically unchanged. Additionally, in the ten years before the war on poverty started, the number of people in poverty was steadily going down. After 1964, the decrease in poverty stopped. The piece of the puzzle that the economics who designed the war on poverty missed is the operation of our programmed poverty consciousness.

> We fought a war on poverty and poverty won. — President Reagan

Poverty often means being in debt. In their happy world of borrowing money most people concentrate on the monthly payments instead of the total debt. They see a $100 payment or even a $200 payment as feasible, but never consider the thousands and thousands of dollars of total debt they will be responsible for. They have fallen into the trap of not saving but instead borrowing money that they may never be able to pay back without declaring bankruptcy. If you continue to carry too much debt, you will never get rich but continue to struggle paycheck to paycheck.

> If you would be wealthy, think of saving as well as getting. — Benjamin Franklin

If you want to become rich, you must not make a study of poverty. Things are not brought into being by thinking about their opposites. Do not dwell on poverty, do not investigate it, and do not concern yourself with it. Never mind what its causes are. Do not think about the poverty of your parents or the hardships of your early life. To do any of these things is to mentally place yourself with the poor. Put poverty and all things that pertain to it completely behind you.

Give your attention wholly to riches. Whenever you think or speak of those who are poor, think and speak of them as those who are becoming rich, as those who are to be congratulated rather than pitied.

> You can complain because roses have thorns, or you can rejoice because thorns have roses. — Unknown

When money and other things reach you, they will come from the hands of others, who will ask an equivalent for them. You can only get what is yours by giving the other person what is rightfully theirs. This is the crucial point where thought and personal action must be combined. There are very many people who, consciously or subconsciously, set their creative forces in action by the strength and persistence of their desires. Yet they remain poor because they do not provide for the reception of the thing they want when it comes. Your negative money habits must be replaced with positive money habits.

> Empty pockets never held anyone back. Only empty heads and empty hearts can do that. — Norman Vincent Peale

Do not continually ask yourself if you are becoming wealthy and achieving your goals. Naturally, you want to see quick results. But give your subconscious mind time to change your old habits and manifest your results. It is counterproductive to seek new results every day or even every week. The largest trees grow from a small seed, and that seed may be on the ground for many months before sprouting and beginning its growth.

PROSPERITY

> Money can't buy love, but it improves your bargaining position.
> — Christopher Marlowe

Many people think that the way to prosperity is to inherit it or marry it or win the Powerball lottery. Of course there is a possibility that you can get money this way, but if you have a poverty consciousness you will probably quickly lose any money that you have won.

There are millions of people who will happily relieve you of your money. In the next chapter, you will see how the gambling industry has made a science of taking your money. Making money and holding on to your money requires that you change your subconscious habits and beliefs about money. It also requires you to be willing to work for your money as all life has always worked for their existence.

If your preference is to be a freeloader, smoke a joint, and take advantage of every government handout program, then you will survive but poverty will be your lot in life.

You may even develop a mindset that it is not fair that some working people have more than you. This negative mindset will color all your following thoughts on money. It will strengthen your belief in poverty and make it all the harder to become for you ever to be wealthy.

A negative mindset causes you to look for all the negative things in your life. Additionally, you don't notice all the lucky and potential positive things that have the ability to increase your prosperity.

> I'm a great believer in luck, and I find the harder I work the more I have of it.
> — Thomas Jefferson

Often, people who come into a lot of money cannot hold on to it. Even multi-millionaires can be caught up in overspending and, before long, end up penniless, or worse, often with millions in debt. Or, if you have negative subconscious issues with money, you may give your money to a Bernie Madoff type of person. He will guarantee you a risk free ten percent profit a year. Unfortunately he was one of those money managers who will manage your money until there is no money left to manage. And then you have nothing. Many lottery winners and sports superstars who had millions of dollars have lost it all because of their poverty consciousness.

If you know nothing about investing, it is a good idea to get financial advice from a professional. But handle the actual money yourself by investing it with a well-known and insured stock broker or bank. If you want to start a business with the money, get professional advice about that type of business and handle the money yourself.

You may now have a poverty mentality, but you don't have to keep it. Your beliefs about money were likely developed early in life, before the age of eight. This early misinformation can remain with you for your whole life. The way we react to wealth and money is influenced by those early beliefs. They can cause negative thoughts and emotions about the subject of money. They can color your perceptions so that you may actually believe that poverty is good or that you do not deserve to be wealthy. But the fact is that wealth is good and you deserve to be rich.

Still, many people are terrified of money and wealth. On one hand, they want to be rich, but on the other hand they believe that they will have to work too hard, or that it is not spiritual, or that it is just plain evil and wrong. Other misconceptions are that wealth means greed or dishonesty, or taking advantage of others. Still other false beliefs are that money cannot buy happiness, money makes you neglect your family, or there are no opportunities left to make a lot of money.

These misconceptions may have found a home deep down in your subconscious mind. These beliefs about money are false but often taken as real by your subconscious mind. Usually you do not even examine them. They are just accepted. They may have given you a low financial self-worth, a poverty consciousness. They may make you resent or envy wealthy people.

POVERTY

> Debt: An ingenious substitute for the chain and whip of the slave driver.
> — Ambrose Bierce

Being broke and without money is not the same thing as being poor. You can always get more money but poor is a state of mind that will keep you in poverty until you learn how to change the conditioning in your subconscious mind.

If you are unhappy with your financial condition, just look at the cause. And the cause is the way you think about money. Your beliefs about money no longer serve you. They obstruct your efforts to become rich. In order to change your financial condition you must first change the way you think about money. Trying to change only your external conditions will not work if you don't change the wrong beliefs.

> When I was young I thought that money was the most important thing in life; now that I am old, I know that it is.
> — Oscar Wilde

What are some of the common negative beliefs about money? The love of money is the root of all evil is a quote from the bible that actually talks about an obsession with money that replaces spiritual beliefs and not money itself. Similar quotes are: money is only made by greedy and dishonest people, and money corrupts.

Then there are concepts such as: you lose your friends if you get rich and you have to work too hard to get rich. These last two may be true, so you have to ask yourself if you are willing to work hard and lose some envious friends, who probably never really liked you, or stay poor and unhappy.

> The way I see it, if you want the rainbow, you gotta put up with the rain.
> — Dolly Parton

It is best not to advertise your money

because there are too many people who would want to relieve you of it. Also, I have found that if you have money you have more time to easily make lots of new friends.

Check out the following list of some common negative money beliefs. If they are your beliefs, these are the things you need to change when you read chapters four and five.

COMMON NEGATIVE MONEY BELIEFS

- Money is the root of all evil.
- If you're rich you are not spiritual.
- All rich people are greedy.
- You aren't good enough to be wealthy.
- Only greedy people are wealthy.
- It's not right to want more than you need
- People with more than they need are selfish.
- Money doesn't grow on trees.
- Money won't buy happiness.
- There's not enough money for everyone.
- You have to have money to make money.
- If you had a lot of money, you would just lose it.
- You don't know about money so you can't be rich.
- It's too much work to be rich.
- There are poorer people who need the money more than you.
- You don't deserve to make a lot of money.
- You're not strong enough to be rich.
- People with a lot of money are unethical.
- You will lose all my friends if you're wealthy.
- Money just causes conflict.

- You will never be able to pay off your credit cards.

This is only a partial list to get you thinking about your money thoughts. Add any other negative money thoughts that you have. Write down all the thoughts that resonate with you. You will use this list in chapters four and five to change your negative beliefs.

We probably all know people who have poor money beliefs, and they depend on government handouts. The ones I know have a very negative money consciousness and believe we should tax businesses more and give the money to them. But the problem is that business doesn't end up paying taxes. They will just raise their prices, lay off employees, shut locations, move their headquarters, or otherwise pass the taxes along to the consumer.

> There is only one boss. The customer. And he can fire everybody in the company from the chairman on down, simply by spending his money somewhere else.
> — Sam Walton, founder of Wal-Mart

It is not important what your past or present situations are. It is not important how many times you have failed in financial matters. You can start now to have a prosperity consciousness.

You have a right to wealth and success. It is much easier to attain happiness and personal development if you have enough money. Very few people can rise to their highest development unless they have money to buy things to use.

Everyone has a right to all the growth they can attain. Since people develop by making use of things, they must have enough money to buy these things.

Everyone's constitutional right to life, liberty, and the pursuit of happiness means they must have the things that are necessary to their spiritual, mental and physical growth; or, in other words, their right to be wealthy. But as Communist and Socialist governments have found, just giving you money doesn't work. If you don't have a prosperity consciousness, the money will soon disappear. But if you do have a prosperity consciousness, then even though you start with nothing, you will attract money.

The desire for wealth is really the desire to attain your dreams and ambitions. It is through the use of material things that a person finds full life for his body, develops his mind, and unfolds his soul. It is therefore of the utmost importance to each individual to be wealthy. It is perfectly right that you should desire to be wealthy. If you are a normal person you cannot help doing so.

You have been told that it takes money to make money. But no one is prevented from becoming rich due to lack of capital. True, as you get capital, the increase becomes easier and more rapid. But no matter how poor you may be, if you begin to understand and use the principles of wealth, you will begin to get rich and you will begin to have capital. Getting capital is part of the process of getting rich, and it is also an inevitable result.

You may be the poorest person in the world and be deeply in debt. You may not have friends, influence or resources, but if you understand and use the principles of wealth, you will begin to get rich.

> I spent a lot of money on booze, birds, and fast cars. The rest I just squandered.
> — George Best

Our future will have many new ways to become wealthy. Homes will be made of concrete, plastic and metal and manufactured by huge building cranes that are actually huge computer driven 3-D printers (additive manufacturing). Naturally the cost of home construction will be reduced. Also the furniture for the home will be 3-D manufactured, again at lower costs. The possibilities are infinite and people involved in this emerging technology or one of the many other emerging new technologies will make millions.

Nanotechnology is another innovation that is already producing many new materials and changing our lives. Today, for the first time, the latest technologies are available to everyone on the Internet.

> We can change our lives. We can do, have, and be exactly what we wish.
> — Tony Robbins

We now live in a world of opportunities for the average person that has never been so great. Only a few years ago, the average person was not connected to the latest science and information. But today, our global communication technology has already transformed many people's lives and will continue to create never-before-possible opportunities. Sure, big government interference and their regulations can slow it down. But even they cannot stop it. The only thing keeping you from participating in this unprecedented prosperity is the poverty consciousness in your subconscious mind. And in this book, you will get the power to change that!

You are not kept poor by a lack in the supply of riches. There are trillions and trillions of dollars circulating in our economy. You are kept poor only by your lack of understanding and use of the principles of wealth.

The entire world is changing quicker today than ever before. Technology, markets, product cycles, outsourcing, and styles are all changing. This change continually opens huge opportunities for people to make enormous amounts of money. Increasing your wealth has never been so easy.

America is at the forefront of this economic revolution. Americans are not smarter than people in other countries, but we are one of the few countries that never lived under the decrees of kings and other dictators. We threw out would-be dictators and replaced them with a constitution from which all other laws derive their legality. We are truly different from Europe and other countries that happily submitted to the dictates of their rulers.

> We are not natively smarter than we were when our country was founded, nor do we work harder. But look around you and see a world beyond the dreams of any colonial citizen. Now, as in 1776, 1861, 1932 and 1941, America's best days lie ahead.
> — Warren Buffett

It is normal to enjoy the marvelous experiences and things wealth can bring us. There is nothing wrong with using your money in this manner. Still, you must remember that it is the uncontrolled desire for these things that puts many people in financial difficulty. Your road to wealth must be balanced. You must be frugal when you need to, but free and easy in your spending when you can afford it.

Frugal does not mean being a cheap Scrooge as depicted in Dickens' *Christmas Carol*. It is important to spend some money on play, vacations, and entertainment. This is a positive reinforcement for increasing your wealth. Your subconscious mind will get this message and work harder to increase your wealth still further.

> If you fell down yesterday, stand up today. — H. G. Wells

To think wealth when surrounded by the

appearances of poverty requires subconscious mind programming. But those who change their old poverty programming are set free from poverty. These people can now conquer fate and have whatever they want.

When you change your old poverty programming and replace it with prosperity programming, everything changes. It is phenomenal. The entire world seems to change with your new reality. Wealth begins with the acceptance of the power of your subconscious thought and your intentions.

> At the moment of commitment the entire universe conspires to assist you.
> — Johann Goethe

How much do you think you are worth? This is a significant question, since many people have a very restricted viewpoint of their value. Most people believe that they are worth a little more than they now have. Very few people believe they are worth a million dollars a year, but you are.

The secret to getting rich is to program your subconscious mind to create your wealth. Think large, but set smaller goals and shorter time periods such as a one-year plan. This way your successes will build on each other.

Chapter Two Greed

> Do you want to spend the rest of your life selling sugared water or do you want a chance to change the world.
> — Steve Jobs

Think large and don't hesitate to ask for a lot. I recall years ago, when I first started working in a new city, I had very little money and spent it all on a few suits for work and could barely afford food, bus fare and a small one-room apartment. In a couple weeks, it got very hot and I realized my apartment had no air conditioner, and I could not afford to buy one.

Using principles similar to those described in this book, I envisioned a clear picture of an air conditioner and a feeling of cool relief. Within a week someone at work sold me a used model for almost nothing.

Then it dawned on me that I did not ask for enough. I still had only a small apartment and I wanted more. Using the principles of wealth, I mentally planned a small house, and within a year I owned a duplex with the rent from the tenant almost paying the note on the whole house. Then with still larger faith, I went on asking for, and getting, even greater things.

> When making less important decisions, I have found it useful to weigh up all the pros and cons. Yet in the case of truly significant matters the decision needs to come from the subconscious, from somewhere within ourselves.
> — Sigmund Freud

If you cannot convince your subconscious mind that you are good enough to be rich, you will never be. However once you read chapter five and program your subconscious mind to your requirements, then it will assist you in getting rich or anything else you want. Your subconscious mind can think of millions of things at the same time. It observes and controls another million things your conscious mind can't. It is really powerful and your subconscious programming will direct its attention to making you rich.

> Prosperity is a way of living and thinking, and not just money or things. Poverty is a way of living and thinking, and not just a lack of money or things.
> — Eric Butterworth

Accept all things you are offered by others, and accept these things with gratitude. It may be that you have no use for these things, but accept them anyway. Always say and mean those magic words, "Thank You." Do not say no when things are given to you. If you do not need the things, you can always donate them to someone else. Accepting everything changes your awareness so that you see more opportunities than you ever did before.

Ronnie Laing said, "The range of what we think and do is limited by what we fail to notice. There is little we can do to change until we discover how failing to notice shapes our thoughts and deeds."

Rejecting anything that the world gives us reduces our ability to see future gifts. When they see a penny lying on the ground, most people ignore it and continue on their way. You must pick up that penny and be grateful for it. This is not about increasing your wealth one penny at a time. It is not an endorsement of the illusion of scarcity. Accepting the gifts the universe gives you allows you to see subconscious connections you hadn't previously known. It is about changing your subconscious thought patterns so that you accept money and other good things that come to you, and more importantly that you accept them with gratitude.

Many people whose lives are good in all other ways remain in poverty due to their lack of gratitude. Having received one gift, they cut the subconscious connection by failing to make their thankful acknowledgment of gratitude.

If it is a new thought to you that gratitude brings your subconscious mind into closer harmony with your goals, consider it well, and you will see that it is true. It tells your subconscious mind that it did well, that you are grateful and to do it again and again. Gratitude will keep your subconscious looking toward the infinite supply of goods and money. It will prevent you from falling into the error of thinking of the supply as limited.

There is a law of gratitude, and if you are to get the results you seek it is absolutely necessary that you should observe the law. The law of gratitude is the natural principle that action and reaction are always equal and in opposite directions. This means that when wealth begins to come to you, do not reject it, and do not waste it. Do not immediately buy more consumer junk. Instead, acknowledge it and show your gratitude by investing some of this money to make more money. This action will cause wealth to continue to come your way.

> Winning is not a sometime thing; it's an all time thing. You don't win once in a while; you don't do things right once in a while; you do them right all the time. Winning is habit. Unfortunately, so is losing. — Vince Lombardi

CHANGE YOUR WEALTH CONSCIOUSNESS

In chapter five you will learn to use **PREP** and **SSSS** to change your wealth consciousness. Your subconscious mind does not distinguish between wealth and poverty. It will manifest either one according to the pictures and feelings you give it. The subconscious mind does not judge things the way your conscious mind does. It just believes the pictures given to it and acts accordingly. It will work to bring you whatever is necessary to make your picture a reality. It will bring you the resources and people to bring your picture to life.

> The Bible has taught us, metaphysics has taught us, myth has taught us, that if you get into the flow, if you do what you're supposed to do, you'll be rewarded with riches you've never even imagined. And so what I have received is the natural order of things. You always, always reap what you sow.
> — Oprah Winfrey

Chapter Three
Gambling Addiction

> Gambling: The sure way of getting nothing from something.
> — Wilson Mizner

There are many negative behaviors that can steal your money and need to be eliminated. Some of them, such as drug or alcohol addictions, are too much to cover in this book, but my future books will cover them.

One of the more dangerous offspring of negative money thoughts is compulsive gambling. It is about the desire for riches while wishing that you did not have to work for them. The difference in results is that someone with positive money consciousness saves and invests his money while the gambler typically loses his.

The desire for money is part of compulsive gambling, but not the main part. It is the emotional thrill and excitement of making a wager and winning money that is undoubtedly at the root of gambling addiction.

Logically we can all see that the cost of building a gambling casino and stocking it with all those machines and tables is enormous. Also, the cost of paying all those casino employees, the utilities, the insurance, the security, the taxes, and returning a profit to the owner is even greater. So logically, we know that the losses of the gamblers end up paying for all these enormous expenses. But still that emotional excitement of winning overrides our logic and we end up at the casino and lose our money. As in most areas of life, emotions can easily win over just logic.

> A racetrack is a place where windows clean people. — Danny Thomas

From our early beginnings, humans have been hunters and fighters, and have always taken risks. It was exciting and those humans felt their adrenaline flow from the fear and anticipation of killing game. Gambling is just another type of risk, and according to archaeologists the first records of gambling date back to about five thousand years ago.

> In the casino, the cardinal rule is to keep them playing and to keep them coming back. The longer they play, the more they lose, and in the end, we get it all.
> — The movie, Casino

Before the growth of the numerous gambling casinos, there were various types of gambling such as card games, et cetera. There were also bookies that took bets on horse races and various sports events. They were often illegal, but law enforcement generally ignored them, especially if the right people were paid off.

The slots, dice, cards, et cetera, are the gamblers' way of trying to make money quickly without giving any consideration for it. But soon it grows into a compulsive, addictive gambling habit and becomes a very complex thing. The gambler can hardly tell why he excitedly follows the actions of the slot machines or the luck of the poker card draw. There is a fever in his blood that drives him, making ordinary ways of making money seem boring in comparison.

A single act of gambling has a guiltless appearance, and the first steps in your gambling career are frequently exhilarating. However, the atmosphere soon becomes upsetting, and compulsive gambling almost always ends badly.

> It's hard to walk away from a winning streak, even harder to leave the table when you're on a losing one.
> — Cara Bertoia

Gaming casinos are designed to bring people in and keep them in. If you stay in one of their hotels, often the only way to your room is to walk through the casino. Look around and typically you will not see any clocks or windows. Everything is designed to get you playing and keep you playing.

Many people say they began gambling for fun, as an escape, to win money, or are just looking for excitement. Some people who gamble on a limited basis, except for leaving a little poorer, do not suffer any serious consequences.

However, other people do eventually develop a gambling addiction.

Gambling may start innocently enough, but often gets totally out of control and often results in a downward spiral. It then leads to serious financial difficulties, unemployment, family problems, job loss, depression, debt, cheating, violence, crime, and even suicide. If you have other addictions or have psychiatric conditions such as bipolar disorder, you are more likely to have a gambling problem than the average person. Unfortunately, more and more legal gambling venues are starting throughout America because of the tax money politicians can get and spend.

If you gamble and lose the money that you need for your usual living expense, you have a gambling problem. Likewise, if you lie about your gambling, can't stop gambling, or can't cope with life without the gambling 'in-the-zone' rush, you have a gambling problem.

> The roulette table pays nobody except him that keeps it.
> — George Bernard Shaw

Slot machines account for about two-thirds of a typical casino's profits. Table games only account for about one-third. Slots may be a game for you, but for the casino it is a seriously big business, and is the number one way that people become addicted to gambling.

'In-the-zone' is the name that is used for a form of trance or hypnosis that—like a drug—

takes over your emotions and controls your conscious mind. Slot machine gamblers in-the-zone become so absorbed that they are unaware of everything else, lose track of time, and often don't even get up from their seat for hours and hours. Unlike most drugs that require increasing amounts to get high, gambling addicts often report that in time they require less playing time to get in-the-zone.

The design of the gambling casino is an area of intense concern to the casino owners in their never ending quest to put the player in-the-zone, keep them there, and take more money from them. Types of sounds, music and acoustic levels, lighting colors and intensities, spacing of machines, the height of the room, and subliminal messages that go directly into the gamblers' subconscious brain are just a few of the variables under intense scrutiny to maximize casino profits. Taking the gamblers' money has become an intense discipline with serious money invested in the studies. Of course, they use an innocent name for this and call it maximizing the players' in-the-zone gaming experience.

> You don't gamble to win. You gamble so you can gamble the next day.
> — Bert Ambrose

Player tracking systems (reward cards) give many casinos unprecedented control over the slot machines from their mainframe computer. At some of the larger casinos, their mainframe computer knows who is playing and is in real time control of the functions of the slot machine's micro-processor that you are using. Often their computer acquires your demographic data and puts it together with your previous playing habits to create a profile of you. Their psychologists have studied many gamblers, and they have programmed the computer with many profiles similar to yours. They know when to let you win and when to keep taking your money. Some computer experts are even doing advance research into eventually putting tiny cameras in the slot machines to determine your emotions from your facial expressions and other tells.

Within seconds of a player beginning, the slot machine the mainframe computer automatically adjusts the slot machine to correspond to the player's profile. For example, one profile is how you like to win. Some players prefer to win many small pots while some prefer to win just a few big pots and some prefer something in between. From your history, the mainframe computer knows what circumstances may cause you to cash out and leave the casino. So their computer adjusts the slot you are playing and lets you get close but then takes those winnings away. The slot machine is instantly adjusted to your taste but you still end up losing your money – all of it.

The loyalty cards that casinos hand out connect you to a central database that records all the pertinent facts of each bet you ever made at the casino. This includes wins and losses, the rate at which you push the slot machine play buttons, when you took your breaks, what drinks and meals you purchased plus much more. Some casinos now use RFID and are able to detect card-carrying players as they move through the casino. This gives their mainframe computer even more information about you.

Using your information their computer can keep you hooked in the zone and excited with your periodic wins. It knows what you need to keep gambling and can send a "Luck Ambassador" to give you complimentary drinks or food or coupons for your next visit.

In the old days they called these machines "one-armed bandits", but in today's computer-controlled world, they are just plain robbers. The gambler who thinks they have enough luck to beat the new generation of slot machines ends up a sadly mistaken mark. You just win when their computer calculates that you need a win to stay in the zone and keep gambling. Eventually, their computer sucks up all your money, leaving you broke but anxious to return another day with more money. Now you know why they call it gaming instead of gambling. It is not a gamble for the casino, since their mainframe computer will be sure that in the long run, they will always win. Welcome to the electronic age of casinos.

> Gambling is a way of buying hope on credit. — Alan Wykes

Gamblers in American put well over one billion dollars every single day into casino slot machines. The power of their mainframe computers allows seemingly random jackpots according to the preferences of the particular players to keep them in the zone and hooked on the slots.

And online gambling is even worse than casinos. Often these web sites originate from countries that offer no rules or regulations as to the "fair" way to take a gambling addict's money. Even though online gambling is accessible from your own home, gamblers tell me it is not as much "fun" as going to a casino. It is estimated that in America alone, people lose a total of about five-hundred-billion dollars a year on various types of legal gambling.

> By gaming we lose both our time and treasure: two things most precious to the life of man. — Owen Feltham

The table games also are controlled so that the house always gets their share. One of the few areas where a gambler can come out ahead (but the casino still gets their share) is the poker table. But unless you have a better method of cheating than they do or have the skills to be a great player, you will lose there also.

There are some poker players that are so good at reading people that they always seem to know about how good your hand is. We all send unconscious "tells" that give these experts their advantage over us. The automatic responses of our body tell the expert poker player all they need to know about our cards. You might call it intuition, but this ability to read your "tells" is well-developed in some people. And yes, the good players often let you win a few small pots before they grab the big ones.

Keeping a poker face is hardly enough. Your whole body tells on you. It is very difficult to hide the hundreds of automatic responses, such as micro facial expressions, eye dilation, and breathing changes. These can all give clues to an experienced player who can read people. It is not logical to think you can really beat the professional poker players, but, as we call their raise, our excited emotions tell us that perhaps this time we can.

Then there are the dishonest poker gamblers who have perfected some technique to get an edge on you. It could be something as simple as having two players at the table passing information. Or it could be something much more complicated. But the bottom line is you lose.

GAMBLING HABIT CHANGE

> The safest way to double your money is to fold it over once and put it in your pocket. — Kin Hubbard

Gamblers Anonymous is based on Alcoholics Anonymous and their twelve-step program. Many people who join it are successful in quitting gambling. However, there are far fewer Gamblers Anonymous meetings than AA meetings, so it will likely be difficult to find a group. To get more information, you can contact them at:

http://www.gamblersanonymous.org.

I have noticed that Gamblers Anonymous provides their groups with the socializing, companionship, and emotional support that you might have not have received elsewhere. Also these groups are an opportunity to lessen your anxiety.

In Gamblers Anonymous, you are encouraged to select a supporter who is an experienced member that you can talk with on a one to one basis. They answer your questions and steer you through the Gamblers Anonymous process.

Due to the fact that membership in Gamblers Anonymous is anonymous, there are no real statistics on the percentage of people it has helped. However, various surveys indicate that about half the people who join Gamblers Anonymous do stop gambling. Some of these people went to professional treatment in addition to their Gamblers Anonymous meetings.

I do recommend Gamblers Anonymous for most people who have a gambling problem. However it is not for everyone and there are a few characteristics that can turn certain people off when they go to their first meeting.

You are encouraged to tell a large group of strangers your confidential, personal problems, and that is difficult for many of us. Some people have difficulty talking in front of groups.

Additionally, though everyone is asked to respect your confidentially, there are no legal penalties for someone disclosing information you divulged at the Gamblers Anonymous meeting.

Standing before a sympathetic group of people who share similar suffering due to gambling experiences is a very powerful way to join a group that is committed to mutual freedom from gambling. This is a significant part of the Gamblers Anonymous method because it combines painful emotions with the support and hugs of a group. You might be able to consider the experience sharing with friends rather than standing in front of a strange group and giving a speech.

One thing that makes Gamblers Anonymous so effective is that many members have quit gambling for multiple years. Consequently, the new members can easily believe that becoming and staying gambling free is feasible.

If you gamble long enough, you'll always lose. The gambler is always ruined. — Michael Crichton

The sounds, the lights, and staring at the spinning wheels while repeatedly pushing the button on the slot machine produce a trance very similar to hypnosis. Since the casino "in-the-zone" experience is similar to hypnotism, going to a hypnotist seems like a reasonable method of removing your addiction. Some people say their gambling addiction was cured by a few sessions with a hypnotist. If you want to use this method, make sure that your hypnotist specializes in gambling addiction and understands it. Experts say that on average it is easier to hypnotize a slot machine player than those of any of the other ways of gambling.

> Lottery: A tax on people who are bad at math. — Ambrose Bierce

There is a positive relationship between gambling addiction and its availability. Various studies have shown that the easier it is to gamble, the more addiction there will be. The additional tax revenue from casinos is certainly not worth our governments addicting so many citizens and ruining their lives.

> There is a very easy way to return from a casino with a small fortune: Go there with a large one. — Jack Yelton

Recognizing that you have a gambling addiction is the first step in learning how to stop gambling. Once recognized, the first goal of your habit change is to keep away from casinos and any other places that have slot machines or any kind of gambling.

Gambling is not a drug, but just a habit and addiction brought on by your many hours of repetitive gambling. Because of the repetition and the environment the casinos created to addict you, a very strong habit was created. Fortunately, you can change the habit and end your gambling addition.

The next goal is to examine the basic motivations of why you started to gamble. It might have been the excitement of wining, your need for money, low self-esteem, depression, a desire to do something different, just boredom or whatever you come up with.

Chapters four and five will show your how to use **CAR, PREP** and **SSSS** to change your basic motivations for gambling. Continue your **SSSS** for at least three months because gambling habits have usually been very deeply ingrained over a long time so it takes longer to change them.

Chapter Four
Habit Change

> Habit is a cable; we weave a thread each day, and at last we cannot break it.
> — Horace Mann (education reformist)

Humans resist change. Often it takes a disease, a crisis, or even a tragedy before we take a serious look at who we are and why we are controlled by our habits. But right now, you have the opportunity to decide to make the changes that will renew your life.

These next two chapters will give you the insights and techniques you need to change your habits and retake control of your mind. Many thousands of habits—both good and bad—control your everyday life. This book gives you the guidance you have been waiting for to help you change your negative behaviors.

A habit can be defined as an activity or behavior pattern that we repeat regularly. Habits are keys in our human ability that render us more advanced than animals. Psychologists also define habits as automatic behaviors triggered by situational cues. Habits make or break us to a far greater extent than we realize. The majority of our many everyday actions are controlled by preprogrammed habits, which can either be positive or negative.

> The great power of habit for good and bad cannot be overestimated.
> — Theron Dumont

Habits make our brains more efficient, allowing us to avoid consciously thinking about routine tasks. Instead, we can concentrate on the newer or more challenging aspects of our current situation.

Habits also are very important factors in our ability to perform tasks quickly and without thinking. A simple example is wearing a seatbelt: most of us buckle up without thinking about it. A more complicated example is riding a bike. Learning to ride a bike requires a lot of attention to balance, and most of us fall a few times in the process of acquiring the skills. But once our subconscious brain takes over and converts a set of actions into an automatic routine, we can ride without ever consciously thinking about balance. Habits can make difficult or complicated things easy.

Habits can also be destructive. They can prevent us from considering why we do something or evaluating if we could do something in a better way. If we engage in a habit over a long enough time period, it becomes a part of who we are, and is therefore that much harder to overcome. You engage in habits subconsciously and often aren't aware that certain actions are actually regulated by a habit. As the saying goes, if you keep doing what you've been doing you'll keep getting what you've got.

Controlling habits is one of the few human skills that are known to produce an extraordinary list of positive benefits in almost all areas of your life. The good news is that you can change any bad habit and get positive benefits.

All of the things that can destroy your life are controlled by powerful habits. Using the instructions in this book, you can take that control back.

You may think that willpower is all you need to change bad habits, but that isn't necessarily true. It works for some people, but just using your willpower to stop many habits is very difficult. One of my professors, when talking about willpower and habits, said that the average person believes he is above average. In other words, most people think they have above average willpower but in fact their willpower is just average. And most people need stronger than average willpower to change a strong habit.

> What you have to do and the way you have to do it is incredibly simple.
> Whether you are willing to do it, that's another matter. — Peter F. Drucker

If you think you have enough strength and willpower to stop a strong subconscious habit like a negative money mind set, then just do it. Many people can temporally stop some bad money habits with their willpower. However, most of us are faced with a continuing conflict between the conscious mind that wants to stop our poverty consciousness and the subconscious mind that wants our long established habits to repeat themselves again and again.

Day after day, month after month, most people will not have enough willpower to constantly fight their negative money consciousness. Eventually, while our conscious mind is thinking about something else, some trigger will occur and cause our subconscious to pull us back into that particular bad negative money habit. This could be a vicious circle with temporary victories followed by temporary and eventually long-term failure.

Instead of simply trying to control your bad habit with willpower, it is much easier to replace it with a better habit. To do this, you need to understand the operation of habits and the operation of your subconscious mind.

> It's the awareness of how you are stuck that lets you recover. — Fritz Perls

Sometimes people are afraid to make changes to their habits. It is the concept of "better to be with the problems I know than those that I do not know." If you have a pet dog, you have probably noticed that the dog is happy with its existing habits and does not like any change; at least until it gets accustomed to the new habit.

The good news about the following habit change system is that if you don't like the results, you can always use the same old money habits you used to have. There is no risk, and you have nothing to lose by changing your habits.

> Nothing is impossible. The word itself says, "I'm possible!"
> — Audrey Hepburn

HOW HABITS WORK

The law of habit states that if you repeat an activity enough, it eventually forms a habit. Once the habit is established, your subconscious mind automatically responds in the same way every time a similar cue arises. For people who do not understand the subconscious mind, resisting it often takes more willpower than they have. Trying to fight or resist the habit usually just entrenches it even more strongly. The next chapter will provide more information on the subconscious mind control techniques that you will use to change your unwanted habits.

> Men's natures are alike; it is their habits that separate them. — Confucius

Pavlov's famous experiment with dogs was one of the first scientific habit experiments that showed the influence of subconscious cues on actions. Pavlov rang a bell as the dogs were given food to eat. Saliva, produced in the mouth, helps in digestion of food. Naturally, the dogs salivated when they saw the food. After a number of bell and food repetitions, the bell was rung without any food but the dogs still salivated. Pavlov discovered that he created a habit in the dogs and the bell alone caused them to salivate.

During childhood, everyone acquires an assortment of various habits that affect them later in life. Some are good, and we want to keep them, but others are bad and negatively affect our lives. These habits are stored deep in our subconscious mind and we often have no awareness of where they first originated.

Like Pavlov's dogs, most of our habits begin without our conscious awareness. We do something and repeat it a number of times, and suddenly it is a habit that began without our awareness.

For example, one electrical engineer I know was having difficulties with his finances. He felt angry and frustrated, and after work used our local gambling casino for zoning out and coping with his stress. After a couple of months, this gambling cycle became a habit, one which he performed every day.

Before he knew it, he was over limit on his credit cards and had a severe money problem. He was stuck in this cycle and felt powerless to make a change. He tried again and again to make a change, but he failed every time. He came to believe that he was powerless to change and was sentenced to a life of financial misery. Eventually, he just stopped trying.

These types of habits can be very difficult to break using only willpower, but you can change them. Your current circumstances and habits do not determine what you can be. Habits can be transformed using the science of habit and mind control described in this book.

> You will be the same person in five years as you are today except for the habits you change.
> — Professor Hal Cohen

In order to change a habit, the first thing you need to do is admit that there is some habit that you want to change. If you spend twice as much as you should on ordering things you do not need, and still think you are doing it to relax from your difficult life, you will not try to change.

CUE, ACTION, REWARD

> Motivation is what gets you started. Habit is what keeps you going.
> — Jim Ryun

Habits are created and can be changed with something called the habit cycle. The habit cycle begins with what's called the **cue**, which acts like an icon on your computer screen. When you click the icon, your computer triggers the associated program. It's the same with your brain when something triggers the **cue**. Then your brain turns on the associated routine to begin a particular habit cycle. For example, the news of someone winning money on the lottery could set off a cue in your mind to buy a ticket for the next drawing. A certain song could remind you of your first love. A certain touch could remind you of your mother's hug. A feeling of frustration, depression, helplessness, and other emotional issues could remind you that going to the mall and buying something nice will make you feel better. These cues activate habit cycles and were probably setup accidentally and without your conscious awareness. But now the habits work automatically whenever the cue occurs.

Some cues can be avoided or changed, but some you can't change. When you take a work break, you may be in the habit of spending a lot of money on something you do not need, but that know will give you a boost. If that is your habit, you will automatically do that whenever you take a break.

The habit cycle is as follows:

Cue ➔ Action ➔ Reward ➔➔➔ Habit Reset

After the cue comes the **action**, which is triggered by the cue. This is the physical action you perform. In the case of taking a work break, the action may be to buy something expensive. You can't change the cue because you need a break, but you can change the action. That is the first key of habit change science. You might find a substitute such as contacting a friend on your smart phone.

Finally comes the **reward**, where you get a psychological or physical reward. The reward is often receiving some type of desire such as pleasure or social acceptance in the work break group. Similarly, it could be relaxing by avoiding the unpleasantness of workplace frustration and impossible targets and requirements. Or it could be the acceptance from your group and avoiding their rejection. Cue, action, reward is a universal method to change any habit by replacing some part of that habit.

A good way to remember the habit cycle is by using the acronym **CAR**. This stands for **C**ue, **A**ction, and **R**eward. You can think of a car that requires you to steer it. Otherwise it will steer itself, causing an accident and possibly destroying your life. Habits are the same, and unless we learn how to steer and control them they will steer and control us.

> You must take personal responsibility. You cannot change the circumstances, the seasons, or the wind, but you can change yourself. — Jim Rohn

Habits are the foundation of many of our behaviors, and most of them were created subconsciously. Understanding the habit cycle allows us to be aware of these habits and gives us ways of changing them. We can use our understanding to create new routines that will change the habit and eliminate the bad or dangerous consequences of the habit cycle.

The great thing about habits is that once you establish or change them, they become practically effortless. It doesn't matter if you're tired or distracted, or have no willpower; the habit still takes over and fulfills your programming.

> Believe you can and you're halfway there. — Theodore Roosevelt

One very powerful key to changing habits is having faith in the possibility that it can be done. Some people might think that changing habits is too theoretical and might not work, but it has in fact worked for many millions of people. If you are dedicated to changing a bad habit, you can trust that this method will work for you just like it has for so many others. Once you understand that we can choose our habits, you will realize that you can succeed in changing them. You can take responsibility for your own life. You can create your own habits.

> We first make our habits, and then our habits make us. — John Dryden

The thing about habits is that you are often unaware they control you. That is why the **CAR** idea is so important. To change a habit, you have to understand how that habit's **C**ue, **A**ction and **R**eward work. It may take some serious contemplation on your part, but the more knowledge you have about the **C**ues, **A**ctions, and **R**ewards of your negative money habits, the easier it will be to change them.

Knowledge and purpose are all that is necessary to change a bad habit. Anyone can overcome habits if they truly want to.

> I can't change the direction of the wind, but I can adjust my sails to always reach my destination. — Jimmy Dean

The easiest link in the **CAR** habit to change is often the action. The other links can be changed or modified, but that is usually more difficult. Sometimes the cue can be modified if you discover that the cue is not what it seems, but the cue is sometimes more difficult to change since it often comes from our environment.

For example, our views on money usually were established at a very early age and are often just there. Our action may be to believe we will just never have money. And when opportunities periodically present themselves, we misread what the environment is telling us and believe that they are not real opportunities and will not work for us.

It is important to understand the habit you choose to change. Break the habit down into the cue, action, and reward. Then think about the action and reward, and determine what rewards you are getting from the action you engage in. The next chapter will teach you how to control your subconscious mind.

> Successful people are simply those with success habits. — Brian Tracy

Make a list of each **cue** that is causing you to lose money. Next to each **cue** write at least one way you can deal with or cope with that **cue**.

If you can't change the **c**ue, the next easiest link in the **CAR** habit to change is usually the **a**ction. The **r**eward can be changed or modified but is often more difficult.

In some cases, the reward might be the temporary relief of your boredom. Removing this reward usually requires a period of enforced abstinence to allow your brain the time it needs to rewire itself and find something else to keep you occupied. Identification of the cue, action, and reward is necessary for the success of the habit change.

You don't need to keep wasting money for excitement. If you slowly but surely reduce your excessive expenditures, you will break their hold on you. If you are unable to do that, then you must use the subconscious mind programming in chapter five.

> Every grown-up man consists wholly of habits, although he is often unaware of it and even denies having any habits at all. — Gurdjieff

As with habits, emotions are stored in your subconscious mind and can sometimes create feelings of anxiety or helplessness. People often cover up these helpless feelings with some comfort shopping spree, buying things that they do not really need or gambling.

Chapter Four Habit Change

> When I shop, the world gets better, and the world is better, but then it's not, and I need to do it again. — Sophie Kinsella

When the shopping is removed, those feelings sometimes return and a different addiction may take its place. If these helpless feelings are very strong, it may be necessary to discover their origins and work to eliminate or lessen their hold on you.

For many people, the origins of these helpless feelings are already known. For others some serious self-examination may be needed. And some will need a few sessions with a professional therapist to get to the root of the problem.

One way to get an insight to the origins of your helplessness is to pay attention to your feelings when you first start to think about spending money for comfort. You may feel inferior, unlovable, unworthy, ugly, uneducated, angry, fed up and so forth. Whatever it is, these are the issues that some people try to escape with spending behaviors. And if you don't examine these issues and work on them, you could possibly begin to escape them by becoming hooked on something else. If this happens to you, use the methods in this chapter to change the new addiction.

It is important to understand the various money habits you choose to change. Break the habits down into their cue, action, and reward. Then think about the action and reward, and determine what rewards you are getting from the action you engage in. The next chapter will teach you how to control your subconscious mind. As we go through the following sections on various life-destroying money habits, you will learn more about your individual habits.

> The greatest things ever done on Earth have been done little by little.
> — William Bryan

The Japanese have a concept called 'Kaizen.' Kaizen is a series of small steps for continuous improvement of something. Companies such as Toyota use it for quality, technology, productivity and company culture. However, it also works for changing your financial habits.

History has shown us that long term habit change is most successful when you focus on smaller and more achievable goals. Often you need to break your habit down into small steps. In other words, instead of trying to throw a football the whole hundred yards for a touchdown, take it in baby steps. Throw a series of shorter, easier-to-catch passes and you'll still get into the end zone.

> I don't look to jump over 7-foot bars. I look around for 1-foot bars that I can step over. — Warren Buffett

Writers use a similar approach because most people just don't know where to start writing a long book. A large number of writers use the

Swiss cheese method, which conceptually entails starting with a solid piece of cheese and taking out a small piece and then another and another until it is completely gone. Once you start at any point of the cheese, you have your foot in the door and you can move forward with writing your book.

> You don't have to be great to start, but you have to start to be great.
> — Zig Ziglar

Breaking up a large habit into a number of smaller habits is an excellent way to overcome your natural resistance to change. Performing a smaller, more manageable habit change still gets you closer to your goal and has other benefits. In addition to beginning your motion towards your larger goal, it increases your ability to change your habits. It is similar to lifting weights; you start out with a light weight and gradually progress up to heavier ones. With habit change, instead of building muscle, you are building the ability to conquer and control your habits.

> If you think small things don't matter, try spending the night in a room with a small mosquito. — Dalai Lama

In addition to compulsive comfort shopping, you can do this with many other money habits such as gambling. Instead of using all your will power to never buy anything you don't really need, you can just change your habit of shopping every Friday to just every other Friday. Then a few months later you can change it to once every three weeks and so on. The reason this works so well is that learning to change smaller habits rewires you brain and makes it easier to change other habits.

BELIEFS

> Champions don't do extraordinary things. They do ordinary things, but they do them without thinking - too fast for the other team to react. They follow the habits they've learned. — Tony Dungy, first black coach to win the Super Bowl

The most important thing about changing your habits is your belief that you can do it. An old quote that describes how this works is "You must believe it before you see it". In other words, you have to actually believe that the habit will change. If you do not believe it, then it is probable that nothing will change. You must be positive and know you can change. With a negative mindset, you will get negative results. Another saying is "if you believe you can change, you can. But if you believe you can't change, you can't."

There is every reason to believe that you can change any habit. In the real world, every single day, untold thousands of Americans change their bad habits and are no longer controlled by gambling, over-eating, nicotine, alcohol, drugs, and all the rest of the major life-destroying habits. These are people from every background and educational level. Smart people can change. Not as smart people can change. Rich people can change. Poor people can change. It doesn't matter who you are; everyone is capable of changing their habits. If all of those people can do it, then you can too. It takes some work, but if you are actually motivated to change and believe you can change, then you will. But you have to want it and believe in it. The good news is that through the techniques in this book, it's possible to change old habits and form new ones.

Motivation, belief, and the techniques in this book will allow you to bring about your change. The next chapter will provide you with techniques to heighten your will to change. It will explain how your mind works. It will give you techniques to redirect internal narratives so you can control yourself and change habits.

> Winning is not a sometime thing; it's an all-time thing. Winning is habit. Unfortunately, so is losing.
> — Vince Lombardi

Once you decide which part of your habit you are going to change, write it down. The act of writing gives additional power to your decision to change a habit. Put the note of your decision somewhere prominent, so that you see it every day. You may want to put it on your calendar or in your wallet or purse. In today's world, you can put it on your smart phone or tablet. I put my reminder in my iPad calendar so it appears every day. You should write down the habit change you want in detail in the present tense, as if it is already accomplished. The next chapter will have more information on why you want to write your reminder in the present tense.

Never make an exception to a habit that you recently changed. For example, to lose a few pounds of weight, I changed my habit of always walking down the grocery store candy aisle (and usually buying some candy) to never walking down it. Naturally, a few days later, I had the strongest urge to walk down the aisle, but my new habit prevailed.

A habit can be thought of as a piece of paper that has been folded. Every time you refold the paper it has a tendency to fold along the same old crease. When we change the habit and make a new crease, the paper will initially easily fold along either the old or the new crease. At that point, a relapse to the old familiar behavioral habit can easily occur. After a week or two of folding in the new direction, the paper has a tendency to fold along the new crease.

It was the same with my candy aisle habit. After a few weeks, the urge to walk the candy aisle vanished. I just naturally avoided it and did not buy the candy that was a major factor in keeping my weight on.

Chapter Four Habit Change

> The great value of habits for good and bad cannot be overestimated. Habit is the deepest law of human nature. No one is stronger than their habits, because our habits either build up our strength or decrease it. — Theron Q. Dumont

You can't always avoid some cues or longings, so make a list of alternative actions you can do to distract yourself for a few minutes. A few of the many possible suggestions are:
- Get up and walk somewhere.
- Turn on some music.
- Phone or text a friend.
- Read a magazine or an Internet article.
- Go to a movie.

> Habit is stronger than reason. — George Santayana

When a business wants its customers to habitually keep coming back, it uses a **CAR** model and adds one other phase to make the habit even more powerful. In addition to the cue, action and reward, they sometimes add investment. For example, if you use Facebook, your investment is in setting up your site with information, pictures and friends. Facebook then becomes a powerful habit that will cause you to sign onto your account more often.

Whenever someone starts a risky behavior, whether it's excessive money problems, gambling, food, cigarettes, drugs, alcohol, or something else entirely, they almost never realize that they are creating a habit and are going to be hooked. If they knew, it is unlikely they would ever allow themselves to become addicted to gambling or even the habit to begin with. But they didn't believe it would happen to them and now they have a problem. The most effective solution is to change the habit.

> If you don't design your own life plan, chances are you'll fall into someone else's plan. And guess what they have planned for you? Not much.
> — Jim Rohn

Summary of Chapter

> A habit is something you can do without thinking - which is why most of us have so many of them. — Frank Clark

In this chapter you learned that the vast majority of life is controlled by habits. Nothing is stronger than habits. Most of them are good habits and let you easily accomplish everyday tasks, such as driving a car while thinking of other things. However, some habits are detrimental, and you would like to get rid of them. Often you can just use willpower to delete bad habits, but sometimes you can't. You learned that particularly difficult habits are easier to change than delete. To change a habit, you have to study its components. These components are broken down into **Cue**, **A**ction, and **R**eward, or the acronym '**CAR**.'

There are some destructive habits that are resistant to the power of your conscious decision to change. This is because long-term habits are stored in your subconscious mind. Unless you understand the way your subconscious works, it is difficult to consciously change long-term, ingrained habits.

The next chapter focuses on subconscious mind control and will give you important facts about your subconscious mind. It will focus on teaching you methods of talking to your subconscious mind and regaining control of it. You can use your subconscious mind to change one of the components of **CAR** and defeat that bad habit. The most important concepts described in the next chapter are the acronym '**PREP**' and the seven step subconscious session to change habits. With these you will be able to use your conscious mind to change habits that are stored deep in your subconscious mind.

> Sow a thought, and you reap an act.
> Sow an act, and you reap a habit. Sow a habit, and you reap a character. Sow a character, and you reap a destiny.
> — Samuel Smiles

Chapter Five
Subconscious Mind Control

> Men occasionally stumble over the truth, but most pick themselves up and hurry off as if nothing has happened.
> — Winston Churchill

Everyone has an unbelievable power, but most people do not know about it. There are numerous things in life you cannot control, but you do have control over yourself and in particular your subconscious mind. You're about to discover the inner workings of your mind and how to control it to your advantage. It will be critical in your habit control, but it will also be important in thousands of other things in your life.

If you do not take charge of your subconscious mind, it will be your own worst enemy. It can easily override your willpower and best intentions. It can dictate your choices for you to blindly follow. It can make your life a living hell. But if you learn to control your subconscious mind, you can easily discipline it to do your bidding and help you eliminate self-destructive money problems.

> Your subconscious is a powerful and mysterious force which can either hold you back or help you move forward. Without its cooperation, your best goals will go unrealized; with its help, you are unbeatable. — Jenny Davidow

You're about to discover how to make your brain's subconscious computer work for you instead of against you. The power to do this is already within you. The simple techniques in this chapter will show you how to use your power and begin a brand new chapter in your life.

The power of your subconscious mind is far greater than you have ever imagined. It is the largest, most complex, and most powerful part of your mind. It has amazing powers, many of which we have still not discovered. There seems to be no limit to what our subconscious mind can do. And we only use a small fraction of our subconscious power.

Your subconscious is where your habits, as well as many other things, are stored. Subconscious mental programming is a wonderful technique that gives you the power to make changes that once seemed impossible. With this technique, you can change your destructive habits and regain control of your life. As you become more familiar with this subconscious technique, you will find that it becomes easier and easier to change all types of habits.

When I was eighteen years old, I took a course in self-defense taught by a really tough and experienced Korean War Special Forces veteran. In one lesson, I was very surprised how important it is to be aware of how my mind works. The particular lesson I refer to assumed someone was pointing a handgun at me. The trainers asked me what I would say. "Don't shoot" was my immediate response, and the rest of the class nodded in agreement.

"Wrong!" said my trainer. "It is extremely likely that the gunman is operating from his subconscious mind and this mind has difficulty understanding negative words or concepts such as 'don't.' All the subconscious hears is 'shoot.' It is far better to say something positive such as 'You win!' This puts the assailant at ease and removes the pressure from their trigger finger."

Next my trainer showed us how to disarm someone who was within arm's reach. He said, "Before you begin the moves that I will teach you, put the assailant in their conscious mind by asking a question." He recommended after saying, "You win," ask the assailant, "What do you want?" Even though I already knew what the assailant wanted, the purpose of this was to ask a question and cause a delay in the assailant's response time when I started the disarmament move. It turns out that the subconscious responds quickly and reflexively, like a computer or robot. The conscious mind can only think of one thing at a time; it takes a little longer to act because it is weighing the various options of the situation. By contrast, the subconscious mind is much faster. It can think of millions of different things at the same time so it arrives at a solution almost immediately and just does it.

We have two different kinds of minds. The conscious mind can decide which course of action is the most logical, but the conscious mind is also relatively slow. The subconscious mind can intuitively complete previously performed tasks, and it is much faster. You can reprogram your subconscious mind to create better ways to do these tasks.

The subconscious mind is the foundation or our lives because it keeps us alive. It responds to threats much more quickly than our conscious mind and allows us to make automatic, split second decisions. It acts to escape dangerous animals or control our automobile to avoid a serious accident. And in addition to keeping us alive, the subconscious mind influences most of our everyday attitudes and decisions on almost everything. As the manager of our many habits, the subconscious mind controls what we eat, how much we eat, what we drink, the drugs we take, and the very health of our bodies. Our ability to regulate our subconscious mind makes all the difference between success and failure in life.

The subconscious mind uses over ninety percent of your brain, while the conscious mind takes less than ten percent. The subconscious mind can do things that the conscious mind has difficulty doing. For example, if you are playing tennis and your opponent is winning, you may want to change his subconscious concentration.

Chapter Five Subconscious Mind Control

One way to do this is to ask your opponent what he is doing differently to be playing so much better today. If he thinks about what he is doing during the next set, he will be in his conscious mind and he may be off his game since he can't react as well or as quickly from his conscious mind. You can try this out yourself by using your conscious mind to think about and do some simple task such as tie your shoe. Your subconscious mind can just do it all day long, but your conscious mind takes longer to figure it out.

I have discovered that the mind behaves as if it had two parts. There is the conscious—or logical, rational—mind, and also the subconscious—or irrational, emotional, instinctive—mind. In almost every sport where quick reactions are essential, the good players are those who respond instinctively from the subconscious mind. The conscious mind can control the software that in turn controls the subconscious mind, but if the software did not come from you but instead was installed by others, the subconscious mind will perform its instructions and override your conscious mind. The physical brain is actually much more complicated, but the two minds concept is all you need to know to conquer and control your unhelpful money habits.

In truth, the subconscious mind is the servant of the conscious mind, but it very often works in the opposite direction. Your conscious mind often goes to sleep and allows your subconscious mind to influence the decisions that dictate your life. Sometimes these decisions cause you to have various addictions that further control your life. When your subconscious mind works against your conscious mind, you will have problems. Unless you know the methods necessary to communicate with your subconscious mind, it will defeat your conscious mind. And the problems your subconscious creates will control your life.

> By learning the laws of mind, you can extract from that infinite storehouse within you everything you need in order to live life gloriously, joyously, and abundantly.
> — Joseph Murphy

SUBCONSCIOUS MIND

As I have stated, the subconscious mind can process information much more quickly than the conscious mind. When a cornerback intercepts a football pass, his subconscious mind is doing the equivalent of solving many hugely complicated equations in just a few seconds. The football's velocity, drop speed, spin and wind direction are just some of the factors. If the linebacker used his conscious mind, the information would not be processed quickly enough and there wouldn't be an interception. The linebacker's years of practice in catching passes have forged the action into a subconscious habit and now it just all works automatically.

Many athletes rehearse their moves in their

mind while they may be far away from the sports field, and possibly even while lying in bed. These rehearsals train their subconscious minds to create habits that perform certain actions as a reaction to certain moves by the opposition. Then when they get onto the field, they don't need to engage their conscious mind; the habits in their subconscious mind kick in automatically.

In golf, many top players imagine themselves making perfect swings and visualize the golf ball falling directly into the hole. These players are in effect changing bad playing habits and replacing them with winning habits. This does not have to be done on the green. Instead, they can practice in their own living rooms using just their minds. Researchers have determined that, even though the muscles do not move, the player's brain waves are identical regardless whether they are on the green or in the living room. When they get on the green, the habits they perfected in their mind magically work to improve their game.

> If we all did the things we are capable of doing, we would literally astound ourselves. — Thomas Edison

The subconscious mind also takes charge of all the things that happen automatically in your body, such as breathing, digesting food and so forth. While you sleep, it continues to remain alert and even generates your dreams. Additionally, it is an enormous hard drive that records the memories of everything that has happened in your life. It is also the seat of your instincts, emotions, creativity and most relevant to our purposes, your beliefs and habits. It is the ideal place to make belief and habit changes.

The subconscious remains only in the present time and not in the past or the future. The conscious mind can be in the past, present or future time. So when talking to your subconscious you must stay in the present tense; instead of saying, "I will be brave," you should say, "I am brave."

> Our subconscious minds have no sense of humor, play no jokes, and cannot tell the difference between reality and an imagined thought or image. What we continually think about eventually will manifest in our lives. — Robert Collier

The subconscious mind does not normally think with words. Instead, it prefers to use instinctive thoughts such as pictures and emotions. The use of pictures and emotions will allow your subconscious to more readily accept your conscious thoughts and programming. If you try to program the subconscious mind using the wrong words, it will reject the programming. Talking to your subconscious is similar to talking to a three-year-old child; you can't argue with it and you have to talk to it using simple concepts.

Your subconscious can't distinguish between what is real and what is unreal. No matter how unrealistic a concept is, if you can get your subconscious to believe the idea it will view that concept as a real fact. Then this new belief of your subconscious will be the new normal, and your life will now turn towards the direction of this new normal.

> For one who has conquered the mind, the mind is the best of friends; but for the one who has failed to do so, the mind will remain the greatest enemy.
> — Bhagavad Gita

As strange as it may seem, your choice of words and thoughts can make all the difference between success and failure with your control of your subconscious mind. But after you learn the language of your subconscious mind, you will be able to accomplish anything that you want. You will be able to take control of your life and change the habits that may now be destroying it.

When your subconscious mind accepts any idea, it begins to execute that idea. It is counter-intuitive but true that the subconscious mind accepts both real and unreal ideas equally. It does not argue like your conscious mind would. It is similar to a computer in that whatever it accepts, it believes. With computers, they say "garbage in makes garbage out," and it is the same with your subconscious mind. Our conscious mind sets limits for us, but our subconscious mind has no limits. It can do what we think is impossible. It can change our habits and free us from our addictions.

Many other people and events have already programmed your subconscious mind, but you are mostly unaware of this programming. You have a lot of garbage in your subconscious mind and you are being controlled by events in your childhood environment. It started when you were just a baby and continued through school and beyond. As a young child, your subconscious mind was aware of most of the things occurring around you, and stored them for future reference. Today, as an adult, this information often affects your thoughts, behaviors, and habits. Some of those habits can be very difficult to change if you don't learn the science of how to reprogram your subconscious mind. A prime example is your money beliefs and habits, which you want to change but your subconscious wants to keep.

Your parents or other authorities may have wrongly told you that you were bad at something. That programmed it into your subconscious and to this day you probably still believe it. You were caught up in that belief, but what you didn't understand was it was someone else's belief that they gave to you. As a child, you had very little choice of what went into your subconscious. Schools, groups, friends, media, and governments continue to exert control of your subconscious habits, with the goal of making you into a more manageable subject.

The good news is that your money problems are probably not your fault. Your subconscious mind was programmed by others and it is likely that you had little or no control over the life-destroying habits that resulted. Your beliefs are just the normal result of your subconscious mind dealing with various feelings of vulnerability that were programmed into it throughout your life. So do not blame yourself for the damaging beliefs and habits that were put into your subconscious brain.

The even better news is that these beliefs and habits can be changed, and practically everyone has had to deal with some bad habits at one point in your life. You no longer have to live your life according to the subconscious programming installed when you were too young to realize its consequences. As an adult, you are free to change or at least update the habits that others have installed into your subconscious. This chapter will teach you how to do it.

> A man's subconscious self is not the ideal companion. It lurks for the greater part of his life in some dark den of its own, hidden away, and emerges only to taunt and deride and increase the misery of a miserable hour.
> —P. G. Wodehouse

The thoughts and images in your conscious mind become the messages your subconscious believes. Do not continue to think of yourself as a victim controlled by destructive habits that were implanted by others. You have the power to modify what you think, how you feel, and what you do. It is your attitude, and not your prior conditioning, that holds you back from being who you want to be. You can reprogram your subconscious and take control of your life. Make the decision to change the behavior you no longer want.

With the assistance of this chapter, you can change the negative money habits, beliefs, and behaviors that automatically come from your subconscious mind. You can determine the habits that control you and choose to reprogram the undesirable thoughts that were put into your subconscious mind. Using the subconscious mind control methods in this book, you can replace those thoughts with the thoughts you want. You can change your life for the better.

> Why be just an average person? All the great achievements of history have been made by strong individuals who refused to consult statistics or to listen to those who could prove convincingly that what they wanted to do, and in fact ultimately did do, was completely impossible. — Eric Butterworth

Much of your childhood subconscious programming is positive, and you will want to keep it. However, a reasonable amount of it is negative, and this negative programming causes various bad habits and unhealthy states of mind that you will want to change. In order to change a habit, you need to use your conscious brain to reprogram your subconscious brain.

One of mankind's greatest discoveries is that you can alter your life by altering your subconscious mind. The only thing necessary for you to do is learn how to get your subconscious mind to accept your ideas and follow up with the subconscious habit change sessions described at the end of this chapter. Then the power of your subconscious mind will bring forth the changes you desire.

Any thoughts or beliefs that your subconscious has once learned can be unlearned. However, if you don't intentionally program your subconscious with the correct thoughts, then it will still be programmed, but the programming will not be in your control. It has already been programmed by others, many years ago, and now it may not be beneficial to you. Understanding your subconscious is absolutely essential to successfully programming it.

Don't mistake this book's subconscious mind programming with simple affirmations. Sometimes affirmations will work, but often the desired habit and belief change does not materialize, even after repeating a statement over and over for months. This is because of weak communication between our subconscious mind and conscious mind. It takes more than just saying some affirmation to make your subconscious believe it is true. You will have to learn the techniques to program your subconscious using the **PREP** method that I will explain shortly.

> Begin to be now what you will be hereafter. — William James

To program your subconscious, it is essential that you perform the **PREP** method of subconscious mind control. Once your subconscious is reprogrammed, it will faithfully work day and night to bring about the requirements of its programming. If your subconscious is correctly programmed to believe that you should be a certain way, it will make it so. The amount of time that you believed your old programming makes no difference; your new program will take over from your old, obsolete program.

The subconscious mind works 24/7 to control all your body functions. It examines all the sensations (sights, sounds, etc.) coming to you from the outside world and then makes sense of them. It is the center of your emotions and inspirational thoughts. Depending on your subconscious programming, your view of the outside world is most likely different than mine. Unlike your conscious mind, which can only think of one thing at a time, your subconscious can think and do many things at the same time.

Your subconscious mind accepts and believes all thoughts correctly impressed upon it by your conscious mind. It is not able to distinguish the difference between truth and untruth. So if you absentmindedly say to yourself, "I'm too dumb" or "I'll always be poor" or "I can't do this" and you believe it, then your subconscious will believe you and make sure you are unable to do it. If you tell your subconscious that you just can't seem to stop maxing out your credit cards, you subconscious will believe you and prevent you from quitting that habit.

Your subconscious mind will always accept your suggestions and will believe whatever is impressed upon it. It doesn't determine if something is good or bad. It doesn't determine if it is true of false. If you believe and think that you are unable to do something—and repeat the thought enough times—then you will not be able to do that thing.

> Whatever we plant in our subconscious mind and nourish with repetition and emotion will one day become a reality.
> — Earl Nightingale

When people greet you, they often ask, "How are you doing?" or something to that effect. Some people answer with, "Not so good today, I'm making it," or even "I'm doing without." Your subconscious is always listening and it will adjust your life accordingly. This is another opportunity to program it either positively or negatively.

Begin today to answer that question with a smile and something more positive such as great, wonderful, terrific, stupendous, fantastic, excellent, marvelous, fabulous, feeling groovy, et cetera. You can even string a few of these adjectives together and after you repeat it enough your subconscious will make it true.

Anyone who wants to change their bad habits and grow as a person should learn how to take control of their subconscious mind. When you do this, both your inner and outer worlds will change according to your wishes. If you follow the procedures and instructions of this book you will achieve the habit and belief changes you previously thought to be impossible. But if you do not learn how to control your subconscious mind, then it will control you and your life will be as someone else has programmed. And it may not be to your liking.

When programming your subconscious, think in positives and not negatives. If you are trying to stop gambling, do not focus on giving up or quitting this activity. All quitting thoughts are negatives. Instead, focus on what you want to do and not on what you don't want to do. In other words, you will focus on changing a habit rather than quitting it. You will tell your subconscious that when the habit Cue comes, it will do a different action that produces a different reward--such as going to a movie, for example. Instead of telling your subconscious that you will not spend more money, use all positives and tell it that you now are adjusting your finances and to be more frugal.

Your subconscious mind never sleeps and is always looking after you. Once your subconscious is reprogrammed, when the Cue comes, you will refrain from absentmindedly wasting money because your subconscious will be alert and enforce your new habit. Like a computer, it will perform the programmed task, and you will be successful.

Your subconscious mind does not work in the past or future; it works in the now. Instead of using words such as "I will do something," use the present tense, which would be "I do something." Use the present tense and your subconscious mind will accept your conscious instructions as fact. Since your subconscious mind only accepts one concept at a time to be true, it will delete any conflicting beliefs and make your new belief its reality. At my university they called this cognitive dissonance. This occurs because of the fact that two contradictory concepts cannot both simultaneously occupy our subconscious. Cognitive dissonance is used extensively in advertising to sell you all manner of things.

> The more intensely we feel about an idea or a goal, the more assuredly the idea, buried deep in our subconscious, will direct us along the path to its fulfillment. — Earl Nightingale

What your subconscious mind believes and expects, your life will manifest. This is the key to changing the various beliefs and actions that control your life.

An example of this is the placebo effect. During World War Two, my father-in-law was a physician in the Pacific theater of war and often didn't have enough medicine to treat the huge number of causalities. He improvised and gave them a pill he said would ease their pain. Sometimes he even injected them with plain sterile water. Frequently the patient's pain improved despite the fact that the pill was just a placebo (a pill without any medication) with no physical effect on their condition. This happens because the subconscious mind believes that the pill or injection is real. It expects it will help to give them pain relief. Expecting pain relief, the subconscious mind blocks some of the pain.

Another difference between our two minds is that the conscious mind tends to be more logical and the subconscious mind is more emotional. The conscious mind is the thinking mind, while the subconscious mind is the feeling mind.

> In the province of the mind, what one believes to be true either is true or becomes true. — John Lilly

CONSCIOUS MIND

Your consciousness is the logical part of your mind. It can analyze, criticize, judge, and choose between various possible courses of action. You will use your conscious mind to program your subconscious mind. Your subconscious mind has many automatic functions, such as keeping your heart beating and controlling your body's breathing. But in this book, we are not concerned with those functions; we are only concerned with how you can use your conscious mind to program your subconscious mind in order to change your unwanted habits. Your subconscious mind is also the seat of your emotions and the storehouse of memory where your habits are kept. We will use the repetition of emotions and pictures to change the habits performed by your subconscious mind.

If you or your environment conveyed

unacceptable habits to your subconscious mind, the surest method of changing them is by communicating positive thoughts—properly directed, of course—to your subconscious. If done properly, your subconscious mind will accept these thoughts, thus forming new and healthy habits.

This is the same thing that many politicians and commercial advertisers do. They use emotions, suggestions, and repetition that your conscious mind may tune out, but your subconscious is always listening and often accepts the message uncritically. The advertisement is not aimed at your logical and critical conscious mind but designed to influence your emotions on a deep, subconscious level. When they repeat the advertisement over and over, your conscious mind tunes it out. But your subconscious is always listening, and when it eventually believes the ad, then the ad becomes your truth.

In reprogramming your subconscious, it is also often advantageous to include harmonious emotions to give more power to the thoughts you use in programming. You know yourself that when strong emotional things happened to you as a child, you still remember them. Do you remember falling down and hurting yourself when you were learning to ride a bike? How about the time you excelled at something and were publicly praised? You remember those things clearly, but you have long since forgotten other less emotional things. So we will often use emotions in concert with positive repetition to change habits more quickly and permanently. If you control your emotional state while you talk to your subconscious mind, you can more easily program it.

You need to understand that you can impress your thoughts upon your subconscious mind to change your beliefs and habits. You can recreate your life and exchange bad habits for good ones. You can become the person you want to be. A few of us can make these changes using mere self-discipline, but most of us do not yet have that power over our minds. We must use subconscious mind control techniques to change our habitual ways of thinking and to modify the thoughts we no longer want. Eventually, as we progress in our programming, it will become easier and easier.

The law of the subconscious mind is that your programming can be changed by your conscious mind when you apply the procedures shown later in this chapter. You are like a commuter programmer: when you properly program your subconscious mind, it will do your bidding. If you let others program your subconscious mind, it will do their bidding.

One important concept you should accept is that you can change your subconscious thoughts. This change can cause your subconscious mind, and then your entire life, to improve dramatically. You should put aside all other concepts and dwell upon this fact until you have fixed it in your mind.

Do not listen to inner arguments against this idea. If a doubt comes to you, throw it aside. If you take your blinders off, even the darkest night will end and the sun will rise. You absolutely can change your thoughts and your life.

When you accept the power of your ability to control your thoughts, everything changes. It is phenomenal. The entire world seems to change. If weeds were planted in your subconscious mind, you can replace them with flowers. Yes, you can turn lemons into lemonade with just the power of your mind.

HOW TO CONTROL YOUR SUBCONSCIOUS

> Before I won my first Mr. Universe, I walked around the tournament like I owned it. I had won it so many times in my mind that there was no doubt I would win it.
> — Arnold Schwarzenegger

When you lose control of your habits and your life, you must reclaim it on your own; you will get little encouragement or advice from your friends. Don't expect anyone to help you. Just follow the instructions in this book and resolve to conquer your weaknesses. No one can do this for you. They can encourage you, they can give you examples of others who succeeded, and they can pray for you, but that is all. You must personally follow the procedures outlined in this chapter. You must do the work. Then and only then will you discover that when your habits are changed, new worlds and realities emerge.

> The secret of getting ahead is getting started. — Mark Twain

If you want a certain result in your habits, hold the image of the result in your mind during your subconscious habit change session, which I will soon describe. Keep your conscious mind positively certain that the correct result will come from your effort. Be sure to picture all the details of this result. After forming your thought, have absolute trust that your expectations are now reality. It is not enough that you want to believe it is possible to get a certain result. You must expect the result and know that it is real.

Your conscious mind can weigh ideas and accept or reject them, but your subconscious mind always believes what it is appropriately told. You do not have to prove or argue or fight about the ideas with your subconscious; it just accepts your conscious belief as true. Once your subconscious mind is programmed and believes something to be true, it controls your life accordingly until it is reprogrammed to believe something else.

The thoughts, pictures, and movies you program into your subconscious mind will become reality in your life. You should never think or speak of the change you want in any other way than as being absolutely sure that it is true and is happening. Be positive and your subconscious mind will accept the desired change as true.

Chapter Five Subconscious Mind Control

> You can complain because roses have thorns, or you can rejoice because thorns have roses. — Unknown

Your first task to increase your control over your subconscious mind is to focus on and express your desire of what you want. Do you think it is best to change the **Cue**, the **Action** or the **Reward**? You have to determine the habit changes you want very clearly and exactly. It should be a very lucid and very real knowledge. You should be able to envision what attaining the change would do for you. See yourself as already having achieved the change. The best place to change your subconscious mind is with your conscious mind. The **PREP** method shown below is the best way to proceed in reprogramming your subconscious mind.

PREP

One of my associates, Bill Malone, came up with the acronym **PREP**. It is a great way to remember the key **Prep**arations that are necessary to program your subconscious mind.

P is for positive. To reprogram your subconscious mind, you have to send it information in a way that it understands. Your subconscious mind works with positive thoughts, pictures, emotions and feelings. It does not work at all with negative thinking. Remember that your subconscious computer has difficulty with negative words or concepts. It is not as discriminating as the conscious mind and will literally believe anything your conscious mind correctly tells it. The subconscious does not respond well to tentative thoughts such as "possibly" or "maybe". Give it positive, definite information.

People almost always use negatives when thinking with their conscious mind. They will say something like "I don't want to be broke", or "I want to stop my money problems". The subconscious mind will not respond well to these statements. A positive statement would be something like "I am wealthy."

When I first heard about positive thinking, I thought it was just some new age stuff. But when I understood that it could be used as a method to program my subconscious mind, it suddenly made a lot of sense.

R is for repetition. You must repeat the instructions to your subconscious mind at least once a day for at least two months. This will be described further below.

E is for emotion and energy. Your subconscious mind pays particular value to a concept when you add strong emotions or passions to your programming words. Even advertisers and politicians use energy and emotions to capture your subconscious and get your sale or vote.

P is for picture. You should visualize that you already have the result you want. Think of it not as a change you want, but as a change you already have. Your mental pictures should be very specific and detailed. The more detailed, the better. For example, if you want to be free of a negative money belief, picture yourself as happily seeing yourself having a large amount of cash in your wallet or in your bank account. You can even turn this picture into a mental movie.

If you want to have a better home, then envision yourself in the new home you want that you want. General concepts may not work, so picture the home exactly as you want it to be. Your movie can be a walkthrough of the house, observing everything exactly as you want it.

Your conscious mind must portray your desired results not in the future, but in the present, as if the results have already happened. Instead of words like, "I want to," or "I will," use words like, "I am," or "I always." Hold your positive pictures and thoughts as already being the truth, and your uncritical subconscious will accept them.

The new or changed habit will quickly become your reality. If your conscious mind believes and trusts that you will change, then your subconscious mind will also believe that and make it so. Picture your habit as already accomplished. The slogan "fake it until you make it" describes the process perfectly. Accept as fact that the changes you want are already reality. If your conscious mind believes it as fact, then soon your subconscious mind will also believe. "Believe it and you will see it," is an expression I heard often during my extensive studies.

Once your subconscious mind accepts your new programming as fact, it will bring this fact into reality and your habit will be changed. You will have reprogrammed your computer and it will now work with you instead of against you.

All belief begins in your will to believe. You cannot always instantaneously believe what you will to believe, but with time and effort your beliefs will change. This must be your first step toward changing your beliefs and habits.

> The thing always happens that you really believe in and the belief in a thing makes it happen. — Frank Lloyd Wright

Your subconscious mind is like a garden, which may be intentionally cultivated or neglected and allowed to grow wild and controlled by weeds. But whether cultivated or neglected, it will grow. If the seeds are taken randomly from your environment, then an abundance of useless weeds will grow, often resulting in destructive habits. But you can tend the garden of your mind and weed out all the wrong, useless and destructive thoughts, replacing them with the flowers and fruits of useful and constructive thoughts. By pursuing this process you will discover that you can change bad habits and actually become the director of your life.

A child's conscious mind develops more slowly than their subconscious mind, and habits acquired in childhood color your interpretation of your personal history. Consequently, you have misinterpreted many of the events that occurred in your early life. These distorted views of your life's events are now habits that continue to affect you today. For example, some adult may have tried to help by rescuing you from a hole you fell in. But the fall was painful and after the event you associate that particular adult with pain. The take-away there is that your past memories may not be accurate and, regardless of what you think your past was, you can use habit change and mind control to write your own future. You do not have to go back in time and correct that error; you just have to change your habits in the present time.

> Any thought that is passed on to the subconscious mind often enough and convincingly enough is finally accepted.
> — Robert Collier

Sometimes when you decide to change your life, you might have a fear of failure that could overwhelm your conscious desires. Again, be on guard not to think any negative thoughts lest they be accepted as true by your subconscious. Do not think about your problems, difficulties, or frustrations. Instead imagine your issues are already solved. Picture how the solution looks and how excited and happy you are that they have been solved so quickly.

The subconscious mind responds well to repetition. This is why to program your subconscious mind effectively; you must talk to it every single day. The subconscious will change to your needs if you send it instructions in a way that it understands. Everyone who puts in the effort of working on themself will be successful.

No matter what you want, envision it clearly with detail. Picture yourself responding in a new way to those poverty thoughts going through you mind. Add feelings of joy and satisfaction when your changed habits obey your wishes.

The subconscious does not reason or judge how your conscious mind decides the truth. It just accepts and believes everything as factual and right. It works to bring your truth to life. The good news is that you can consciously overcome habits and control and rewrite your subconscious mind to work for you and not against you.

> Nothing great was ever achieved without enthusiasm. — Emerson

Set up at least one regular time every day for your subconscious programming session. This way you make these sessions a routine and then a habit. In the evening just before bedtime is best. Next best is when you first wake up. These are preferred since at these times your subconscious is most susceptible to thoughts impressed upon it by your conscious mind. Another good time is just before or after a nap. Any regular quiet time of the day can work, but immediately before or after sleep works best. Many people have found that using an event, such as going to bed, works better than just using a clock time. In our busy lives, unexpected occurrences can disrupt our plans for programming at a specific time, but we go to bed virtually every day. The most important thing is to be regular and not to allow any excuse to keep you from your session.

Repeating something often enough causes your subconscious mind to believe it. This is the reason advertisers show the same commercial over and over.

At the end of your session, be grateful that your new reality is already here. This gratitude is perceived by your subconscious as further proof of what you want, and it will work harder to bring your desires to completion.

> Gratitude makes sense of our past, brings peace for today and creates a vision for tomorrow. — Melody Beatti

Reprogramming your subconscious is similar to building up your muscles at the gym. If you want to eventually lift 300 pounds, you might have to start with 30 pounds and work your way up. Training your subconscious is the same: you often have to start with just a part of the total change you eventually want. Every time you consciously reprogram your subconscious it becomes easier and easier.

> The difference between try and triumph is just a little umph! — Marvin Phillips

SEVEN STEP SUBCONSCIOUS SESSION (SSSS)

Following are the instructions to program your subconscious mind. In the beginning, it might take you ten minutes or more. With a little practice, it will take seven minutes or less. Everyone who really wants to change a bad habit can find this small amount of time to completely change their life for the better. As I said above, the best time to do this is just before going to sleep. The transition between your waking state and your sleeping state naturally allows you better communication with your subconscious mind. Make sure you are in a place where it is unlikely that anything will disrupt your attention.

> If you accept the expectations of others, especially negative ones, then you never will change the outcome.
> — Michael Jordan

SEVEN STEP SUBCONSCIOUS SESSION

Step 1. To begin your **S**even **S**tep **S**ubconscious **S**ession, write down the habit you want to change. Use the principles of talking to your subconscious mind and write it in a present, positive, and already true way. If you are working on overspending, an example would be "I am calm, relaxed, and love to save my ten percent every paycheck." Because of our formative years in elementary school, our subconscious elevates the written word above other thoughts and accepts it as truth. Handwriting works much better than typing.

Step 2. Sit or lie down, relax, and close your eyes. With your eyes still closed, roll them upward as if you were looking at the top of your forehead. This is a very important step that helps your conscious mind communicate and join with your subconscious mind.

Step 3. Inhale slowly, deeply drawing air in, and then exhale just as slowly. Let yourself relax as you exhale. Focus your attention on your breathing. Listen to the sound of the air going in and out of your body. Allow yourself to relax as you slowly breathe. Do this for three complete breaths. These three deep breaths increase your conscious control of your subconscious mind.

Step 4. Now, with your eyes still closed and still looking upward, speak or think the positive message you wrote down and want to implant into your subconscious. Say "I am calm and relaxed, and money is my friend."

Change and adjust the words and images to control the habit of anything you are currently working on. Again, notice the message is in the present tense—"I am"—and not the future tense.

Step 5. Using sensory-rich details, visualize a picture or make a mental movie of your message. See yourself in all the detail you possibly can. Hear the sounds of your coworkers or friends talking. Smell the fresh outside air. Feel the happy thoughts of being free from your old problems. Try to use as many senses as possible to give substance to your vision. Whatever your goal is, see it as clearly as possible. Make the image crystal clear. Give your vision as much detail as you can. In your first session, there may not be a lot of detail, but as the days go by, you will be able to add more details to your vision.

Step 6. Add emotional content to the positive results. Recall something in your life that made you very happy. This may be a time when you achieved some huge success or some enormous win. It does not matter when it occurred but it must be something that made you feel genuinely happy. Relive the happy emotions of that wonderful past event. Re-experience the good feelings as if they were happening now. Recall your emotions as vividly as you possibly can. Now with those wonderful feelings, continue to repeat your subconscious statements you wrote down from step one.

Step 7. Relax and feel that the picture you created is now an actual fact. See yourself as already owning this habit change. Feel the thrill of your success in altering your belief or habit. This is your new reality, so now open your eyes and give gratitude to the wonderful world that gave you this power. Gratitude is very important, since it signals to your subconscious that you have now completed this change—that the change is real and is your actual present reality. Your subconscious will then find a way to fulfill this reality.

> Whatever the mind of man can conceive and believe, the mind of man can achieve. — Napoleon Hill

Upon completing your Seven Step Subconscious Session, take a minute or two to examine any ideas you might have had to improve your next session. For example, your subconscious mind may have given you feedback about something that might give you an insight about a cue, action or reward you are working on. If so, jot it down and adjust your next session to incorporate the new information.

The **S**even **S**tep **S**ubconscious **S**ession has linked happy feelings with change images and implanted them directly into your subconscious mind. This will cause your old habit to be replaced with your new visions.

But one session is definitely not enough. Your old habit may have been in control for years and years, so it will take time to permanently change it.

It's not enough to just want to improve your money situation or to just believe that you deserve more money. You have to do the work necessary for that money to materialize. Daily work on your subconscious mind plus perseverance is required.

I know that I am repeating myself, but you have to be prepared to repeat these sessions for about two months. Everyone's time varies depending on the habit and your motivation. Some people can change a habit in a few weeks, while for others it may take six months. It also depends on the particular habit and your experience in habit change. If this is your first try, it may take longer. Later it will take less time. Additionally, a very strong habit will definitely take longer than a weak habit. Don't be discouraged, though; with patience and dedication, you can completely turn your negative money or gambling habits around.

Notice that in this example, we used a **P**ositive statement, "I am calm and relaxed, and money is my friend" instead of "I will stop having money problems." The **R**epetition is daily for at least a month or more. The **E**motion is to recall something in your life that made you very happy. And the **P**icture is to see the eventual results as your present reality. See it in all the detail you possibly can. You can also include hearing and feeling senses. Your mental pictures should be very detailed; the more the better. It can even be a mental movie.

The methods here are for people whose desire for change is strong enough to overcome laziness and do the **S**even **S**tep **S**ubconscious **S**ession. A daily commitment is necessary. With this commitment, you must have an unwavering faith (fake it till you make it) that the habit is already changed and all you have to do is recognize it. Repetition is the key.

Again, what you have to do is form a distinct mental image of the goal you want. The goal comes from the belief or habit you are changing. Also, hold fast to your purpose and be positive that your results will be forthcoming. Even if at first it takes more than two months, keep your positive attitude; if you do not believe, then your subconscious mind will not believe and it will resist change.

> There is no chance, no destiny, no fate that can circumvent or hinder or control the firm resolve of a determined soul.
> — Ella Wheeler Wilcox

In your **SSSS**, allow yourself to see the things that you want to come to you. If you want a large house on the beach, see the house in all the detail you possibly can. Hear the sounds of the water. Smell the fresh breeze. Feel the warm golden sun. Try to use as many senses as possible to give substance to your vision. Whatever your goal is, see it as clearly as possible. Make the image crystal clear. Give your vision as much detail as you can. In your first wealth reality session, there may not be a lot of detail, but as the days and weeks go by, continue to add more details to your vision.

See yourself as already owning this fantastic house. Walk through it knowing that it is yours. This is your house, so now open your eyes and give gratitude to the wonderful world that gave you this house.

I used the example of a large house because that is the desire of many people. There are numerous other things that you may want. Some people do not want a house, but just want money, cars, or things, and the freedom those bring. Whatever you want, be sure to envision it and attach positive emotions. If you want money, you might see yourself sitting on piles of hundred-dollar bills and feeling the joy and freedom of not having to go to the office again.

> The seven deadly sins . . . food, clothing, firing, rent, taxes, respectability and children. Nothing can lift those seven millstones from man's neck but money. And the spirit cannot soar until the millstones are lifted.
> — George Bernard Shaw

What habits and subconscious beliefs sabotage your ability to be wealthy? There are hundreds of negative money beliefs as shown in chapter two. Do any of the following beliefs sound familiar? Money doesn't grow on trees. Money is the root of all evil. You have to be dishonest to make money. You can only be successful through connections. My family and friends won't like you if you get rich. If you were meant to be rich you would be rich already. You don't deserve to be rich. Happiness and money are incompatible. Money is dirty and corrupts you. Rich people can't be trusted. The more you have, the more you'll want.

If these or similar beliefs control your subconscious, use **PREP** and **SSSS** to change them. Change these negative beliefs to positive beliefs such as: "Money is good," "I am wealthy," et cetera.

Remember that your present circumstances don't determine who you are or what you can do. It is never too late to begin to become what you might have been. Reprogram your subconscious thoughts, and you will change your world.

Chapter Five Subconscious Mind Control

> Once we open our eyes to the infinite magic that the universe has in abundance, we are sure to be enthralled by what we see and this miraculous creation gets us closer to our dreams and to the world as a whole.
> — Stephen Richards

Things that dominate our thoughts also dominate our beliefs. If you want to become wealthy, you shouldn't study all the additional credit cards that you can get and go deeper into debt. Things are not brought into reality by thinking about their opposites.

Doubt and unbelief are as certain to start a movement away from your goals as faith and purpose are to start one toward them. Every minute you spend giving power to doubts and fears, every minute you spend in worry, every minute in which you are possessed by unbelief sets a current away from your goal of changing your habits.

> Destiny is not a matter of chance, it is a matter of choice; it is not a thing to be waited for. It is a thing to be achieved.
> — Winston Churchill

Do not argue with your subconscious mind. Remember that your subconscious is like a computer. You do not argue with your computer program. You know that your computer will not do something it was not programmed to do. You have to update your applications to get the functions you desire. It is the same with your subconscious mind.

Once your new money beliefs are established, they specify how you now view the reality of money. These beliefs result in a self-fulfilling prophecy where your net worth continues to increase.

A self-fulfilling prophecy is the result you get after you do the simple exercises in the habit and subconscious mind chapters of this book. Basically, you are directing your subconscious mind to work with your conscious mind to explore your idea. Refinements to your idea are attracted to you because your subconscious mind is always working and is so very powerful and you directed it to work on that idea.

> What lies behind us, and what lies before us are small matters compared to what lies within us. — Ralph Waldo Emerson

Use the instructions in this chapter to control your subconscious. Repeat the **SSSS** exercise once or possibly twice a day. These seven steps may seem strange to you, but our subconscious mind is strange. We can either control it or it will control us. I choose control over my subconscious, and I hope you choose the same.

Your subconscious believes that the written word is official and real. In step one of the **Seven Step Subconscious Session**, you wrote down the habit you want to change as if it were already accomplished. Keep this paper in your wallet or purse until this habit change is established.

Computers and smart phones now have a number of programs that track and assist in forming habits. I believe that paper and pen work better, but some people prefer to do it digitally. If you are one of those people, do some research and find an app that works for you.

> There is a tide in the affairs of men, which, taken at the flood leads on to fortune. Omitted, all the voyage of their life is bound in shallows and in miseries.
> — William Shakespeare

You may think that change in your life should happen in the way that you expect, but often it's the opposite. You may try to change one part of your habit in a certain way but find that another part changed. Regardless of the exact change, your bad money habit will have been fixed.

Something might happen that you think is bad, but it will open new doors for your success. Do not be concerned about how things arrive; instead, hold onto your vision and follow the principles of subconscious mind control, and everything will end up in its place.

The power of belief is utterly fantastic. For all of recorded history, it was believed that humans were physically unable to run a four-minute mile. No one did until 1954. Then along came Roger Bannister, who not only believed it could be done but actually did it. That was great, but the amazing thing is that once people realized that four minutes was not a physical barrier but just a subconscious belief, everything changed. Within the next year, thirty other people had also run a four-minute mile. Before 1954, no one could. By 1955, 31 people had.

For difficult habits, it sometimes helps to tell someone or some group about the change in your life. This is especially true for social people who are usually in groups or on their smart phones instead of by themselves. But never share your habit change progress with envious or negative people. Your subconscious mind will hear their negative response and possibly believe it. Only share your progress with positive, supportive people who will encourage you to continue your quest to conquer and control your habits.

Long ago, when I first started writing, I shared my hopes and thoughts with someone who said that I would never be published, and he explained why. It bothered me for a while, but I overcame it and this is now my sixteenth book published by a variety of publishers.

> There is a track just waiting there for each of us, and once on it, doors will open that were not open before and would not open for anyone else.
> — Joseph Campbell

Most people are controlled by their subconscious and driven by the insecurities, vulnerabilities, and inadequacies in their life. They are passengers on the road of life and not drivers of the car. If you're not in the driving seat, you're being controlled or subjugated by the mental programs that you have accepted without even knowing it. You don't have to be subjugated by the mindless conditions that would rule and control you. If you use your conscious mind to reprogram your subconscious mind, you will no longer allow people or conditions to take advantage of you.

We all have worldly desires, and the subconscious mind directs us to do whatever it takes to fulfill these desires. You can rise above the programming and be free to choose your destiny.

Yes, it's easier to just go along with the crowd and do what they're doing, but you'll end up exactly like they are. You will be subjugated. You will be one of the masses; a cog in a wheel, a digit in a computer.

Psychology and money are the two main tools that people use to control you. But you don't need approval from others if it results in their control of you. Also, you don't need conventional status symbols, such as a two million dollar house or the finest sports car.

> Laugh and the world laughs with you; cry and you cry alone. — Unknown

Some years ago, a study was performed to demonstrate how controlled we are by social norms. The participants were divided into three groups. Group one was told that they would hear a joke and to behave as if it was a great joke.

Groups two and three were not told anything. Groups one and two were put back together and after hearing a really bad joke group one laughed as they were told, and many in group two also began giggling and feeling surprisingly euphoric. As a control, group one was then told next time not to laugh at the joke. Groups one and three were put together and the same bad joke was told. No one laughed, and the joke bombed. It was the same joke but no one in group three laughed or thought it was a good joke. This is the same concept as the laugh track often played on TV comedy shows: the laughing from the TV show causes many viewers to be more prone to laugh.

You can use this concept by yourself; your behavior can create your emotions that are useful in the habit change exercise. Purposely tell yourself to smile and will you feel happier. Tense your muscles and pretend that you are vulnerable and in danger, and you become uptight and more focused on the present moment.

> It is never too late to be what you might have been. — George Eliot

I remember when I was a young man and a huge football player had words with me. Then he made a fist and took a swing at me. My subconscious mind took over and all I did was perform a very small action than had previously become a habit due to my training over and over in this precise move. I instinctively parried and, keeping contact with his arm, I pulled it. At the same time, I took a step backward. He was off-balance due to the force of his swing, and I pulled him forward down hard. He hit the concrete ground with a very loud thump. He knocked himself out and didn't move. I looked around and saw he had a few friends, so I made a very quick exit. Due to many hundreds of repetitions, that one small step and pull became a habit in my subconscious mind and it saved me from what might have been a very dangerous situation.

> Magic is believing in yourself, if you can do that, you can make anything happen. — Johann Goethe

If you are just starting out with habit control and trying to make a huge change but are having difficulty, then take things one small step at a time. Just the smallest actions can make a big difference in your life. You don't have to go for the home run; just get on base.

> Nothing is particularly hard if you divide it into small jobs. — Henry Ford

In China, there is an old saying that "a journey of a thousand miles starts with a single step." Steve Jobs used this concept with his computers, iPods, iPads and iPhones. He came out with a great innovative product and continued to improve the original model, making it better and better.

Often, changing a big habit seems

overpowering, so the solution is to break the habit down into a number of smaller changes. This develops the awareness that change is possible and strengthens your habit control. As you see the success of this concept, move ahead and change other habits until you complete all the changes you want.

> The great thing in the world is not so much where we stand as in what direction we are moving.
> — Oliver Wendell Holmes

After you change your unwanted negative money consciousness habit, you may find that the psychological emotions your habit covered up are now exposed. It is good to pay attention to these exposed emotions because this gives you an opportunity for a deeper understanding of what issues drove your unwanted negative money habit. Some people have found that these exposed emotions are redirected into other areas of their life. However, subconscious mind programming is also effective in eliminating the underlying issues and emotions that drove your habits in the first place.

Often there are social habits that reinforce addictions. For example, if your social life revolves around a group where everyone has a negative money consciousness, you will need to change your social life and the places you frequent. Fortunately for you, your subconscious mind programming works on this as well as on the money problems.

> Habit is habit, not to be thrown out the window by any man, but rather coaxed down the stairs one step at a time.
> — Mark Twain

Negative money beliefs are habits that are often associated with underlying emotions stored in your subconscious mind. Traumas, childhood abuse, neglect, violence, vulnerability, and emotional distress are some of the occurrences that produce these destructive habits. This is why we reprogram the subconscious and change these unwanted habits.

> Knowing is not enough. We must apply. Willing is not enough. We must do.
> — Johann Goethe

SUMMARY OF THE CHAPTER

The only thing that could stop you from realizing the dream of changing your life-destroying negative money consciousness is procrastination. Procrastination means putting off something that you know you should do because of fear of change, avoiding confrontations, avoiding responsibility, or some other belief or feeling that drives you to maintain the status quo.

I am here to tell you that the habit change technology from chapter four combined with the subconscious mind control in this chapter is almost magic. It will lift your life to the next level where you will be free of the poverty habits that are slowly crippling your energy. The only real thing that keeps you from taking action is you. You owe it to yourself to move beyond procrastination and take control of your life.

> I've failed over and over and over again in my life, and that is why I succeed.
> — Michael Jordan

Jane had a difficult boss at work, and every day he criticized her. One of her coworkers was laid off and Jane was expected to take up the slack. Jane felt helpless and could barely make it through the day. She thought about quitting and getting another job, but it was a difficult job market, the economy was bad, and her pay was good. She knew that she was helplessly trapped. So to relax, she stopped by the gambling parlor she passed on her way home. This temporally took her mind off her problems and made Jane feel better, but she could actually see her checking account getting smaller and knew she had to change her habits.

Jane examined the **CAR** of her habit and knew her boss wouldn't change so the **C**ue would be difficult to change. She also knew she needed some reward after work to make up for that terrible boss. So that left the **A**ction as the best bet to change. Her husband's health club had an elliptical machine, so on the way home she stopped in and used it for half an hour. It worked and she was able to skip the gambling and take her anger and frustration out on the machine. On one unusually difficult day, however, her old **CAR** automatically drove her back to her old habit.

Jane knew it was time to use the **PREP** method to permanently change her action regarding gambling. So for **P**ositive she decided on "To relax after work, I use the elliptical exercise machine." For **R**epetition, she used every evening while lying in bed just before she went to sleep. Because of her anger at work, the Emotions were easy. She just imagined that peace and serenity surrounded her when she walked on the machine. Finally, for the **P**icture, she envisioned herself as if in a movie, exercising on the elliptical machine and relaxing into a peaceful state.

She used this movie in her **S**even **S**tep **S**ubconscious **S**ession. First she wrote down that after work, she would use her elliptical machine to relax. Then every night as she was falling asleep, she rolled her eyes upward and slowly took seven breaths. She spoke the words she wrote on the paper and envisioned herself using the elliptical machine while being in a relaxed, peaceful state. She recalled the joy she felt when her father taught her to ride a bike and saw her actions as real and true. Then she gave thanks for the peace and comfort the elliptical machine gave her. In the days that followed, the old gambling habit was magically and permanently changed into the exercise habit.

FLOW CHART OF JANE'S PROCESS

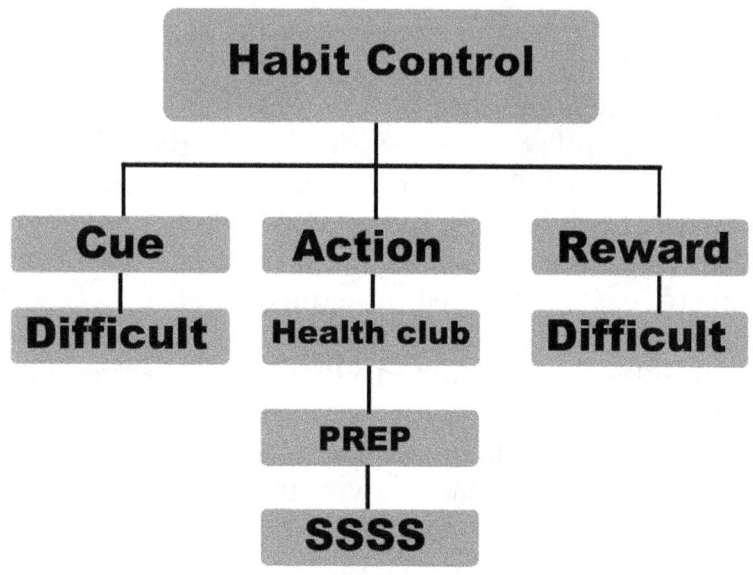

In this chapter, we learned the **PREP** technology. You can use **PREP** to change one of the components of **CAR** (from the previous chapter) and defeat the habit that is destroying your life.

<u>P is for positive</u>. Your subconscious computer has difficulty with negative words or concepts.
<u>R is for repetition</u>. You must repeat the instructions to your subconscious mind at least twice a day for at least a month or two.
<u>E is for emotion</u>. Your subconscious mind places particular value on a concept when you add strong emotions or passions to your

programming words.

P is for picture. Your mental pictures should be very detailed. The more detailed the better.

"Fake it until you make it," is a memorable slogan that describes the concept. Accept as fact that the changes you want are already reality. If your conscious mind believes it, then soon your subconscious mind will also believe. Once your subconscious mind accepts your new programming as fact, it will make that fact reality and your habit will be changed. You will have reprogrammed your computer, and it will now work with you instead of against you.

Do not be overly alarmed if you have a few relapses into your previous habit pattern. Just continue to faithfully do your subconscious mind reprogramming and you will soon be completely successful.

Conclusion

> Your resistance to change is likely to reach its peak when significant change is imminent. — George Leonard

In chapter four you learned that a habit is a **Cue**, an **Action**, and a **Reward**. Often, a habit can be changed by just changing one of these three components. Usually your willpower and the knowledge of how habits work is all you need.

However, some habits are difficult for most people to change with just willpower. Your conscious mind controls your willpower. If you decide to stop a long established habit by relying solely on willpower, you could easily fail. This is because your habits are stored within your subconscious mind. The subconscious is much more powerful than your conscious mind. After a few weeks your willpower may wane and if you have a weak moment, you can easily return to your old way of thinking. Since habits are stored in your subconscious mind, and it is easiest to change them there.

To reprogram the subconscious, you need to know how to communicate with it. You learned to use **PREP** which stands for **P**ositive, **R**epetition, **E**motion, and **P**ictures. Then you learned how to perform your daily subconscious mind programming called the Seven Step Subconscious System.

In this book, I focused on money consciousness and gambling. However, there are literally thousands of additional habits that you may want to change. The **CAR**, **PREP**, and **SSSS** instructions will allow you to change them.

My other books in the Conquer and Control series are located at the website:
http://www.conquerandcontrol.com.

They show you how to change many other habits using similar techniques. Additionally, I am writing other books to add to the Conquer and Control series.

Some of these habits are certainly minor, but you can still change them. For example, my physician told me to cut down my coffee drinking to eliminate my stomach pains. I easily went from eight cups a day down to just one. I probably could have done this with willpower, but it was easier to just let my subconscious mind take care of it.

> In any family, measles are less contagious than bad habits.
> — Mignon McLaughlin

If you are a student, you can change your study habits. If you fear public speaking, you can change that habit. The possibilities are endless. In the future, I will have more detailed information on changing some of these habits at:
http://www.conquerandcontrol.com.

Subconscious programming can also be used to switch off various abnormalities that cause pain. However, you should first consult your physician, because pain can be an indicator of a disease that requires treatment.

ABOUT THE AUTHOR

Alan Fensin began his career with Boeing and NASA in the early days of the American space program. He was a key member of the Apollo rocket design team that successfully put a man on the moon. As an electrical engineer, Alan helped design many of the critical elements used in the electrical system of the Saturn 5 moon–rocket. Returning to school in 1976, he earned an MBA from Tulane University, majoring in Behavior Analysis.

During the early 1990's, he discovered the *Conquer and Control* concepts and this system for using the subconscious mind to change unwanted habits. He believes that this knowledge changed his life, exposing and dealing with money problems that had previously limited his growth.

He has been a lecturer and writer for the last twenty years.

www.ingramcontent.com/pod-product-compliance
Lightning Source LLC
Chambersburg PA
CBHW061949070426
42450CB00007BA/1096